ENDORSEMENTS

Revival hubs dwellers are well diggers. Jennifer LeClaire and Ryan Lestrange have tracked down and uncovered live expressions of the church the world is dying to see: the church-as-we-have-never-known-it, the church restored to its original blueprint. They call what they have been observing and working atRevival Hubs. Here's how they define it: a center that is focused on digging and maintaining a rich well of revival and Spirit-led ministry unto equipping, awakening and societal transformation. If you're among those who are thirsty for what the Holy Spirit is doing right now on this planet, this book is a must! LeClaire and Lestrange are creating langage to communicate the shift that's overtaking the Christian world.

Alain Caron,
Author of Apostolic Centers
Founder and director of Hodos Apostolic Network.

****

God is raising up a new wineskin that will be able to receive, steward and sustain a fresh move of His Spirit in the earth. As a travel minister I get to see a trans-local, international perspective of the body of Christ. There are many churches and pastors in this hour transitioning from a traditional church model into apostolic centers with the vision shifting from simply gathering sheep together, to equipping, empowering and sending the body of Christ out to impact the world around them. It's a shift from inward focus to outward focus. God wants to invade whole cities with His glory, just like He did with Peter in Acts 5. God is raising up habitations for His glory that will impact entire cities and regions with the Kingdom of God. In

Revival Hubs Rising, Ryan LeStrange and Jennifer LeClaire not only prophetically communicate what God is doing in this hour, but also share crucial insights into how to see these apostolic centers of God's glory and power established in your city and region. I recommend this book for every leader and believer who desires to be a part of the new wineskin God is forming. It's important that we continue to move with the cloud of God's presence so we don't become empty structures void of power. I believe as you read this book, God will give you creative strategies to seeing His Kingdom advance through your life and ministry.

Matt Sorger,
Prophetic Healing Revivalist, Author, TV Host
Matt Sorger Ministries
www.mattsorger.com

****

Revival hubs. What a word for today. The Holy Spirit began to show me several years ago a coming wave of revival in which the church will see billions of souls coming into the Kingdom. I often thought, "How will we be able to accommodate such enormous growth? Is the church prepared for what the Lord is about to bring to planet earth? Can we disciple such a vast number of souls coming to Christ?" This book helps answer these questions. With many planning for a doomsday destruction others are carrying keys to the Kingdom. Preparing for Kingdom growth is essential at this time. The keys of the kingdom in this book is planning for a Third Great Awakening, an explosion of harvest like never before and a way to disciple those who come to Christ. I whole heartedly recommend that you read this book by my friends, LeClaire and LeStrange from cover to cover, then buy several for your friends.

Ken Malone

Apostle

Forerunner Ministries

****

The Joel 2 and Acts 2 End Time Outpouring is a prophetic certainty that is already being manifested in the earth and will soon sweep across the US. Revival Hubs Rsing is a divine blueprint and handbook given by the Holy Spirit to the body of Christ through Ryan LeStrange and Jennifer LeClaire that shows you how to steward and maximize this glorious unprecedented move of God. God chose Ryan LeStrange to release this because He is this! If you believe in awakening, revival, miracles, and supernatural power as the means to national and global harvest, this book is a must read!

Eddie James

Founder of Eddie James Ministries

REVIVAL HUBS RISING

REVEALING A NEW MINISTRY PARADIGM FOR THE NEXT GREAT MOVE OF GOD

RYAN LESTRANGE

JENNIFER LECLAIRE

Dedication

This book is dedicated to every revivalist in every age. We honor the men and women in our generation that have made intercession and labored for awakening, and we bless the young revivalists who are rising up in this hour.

CONTENTS

Foreword.....iii

1. Revival Hubs Rising.....1

2. What is a Revival Hub?.....9

3. Comparing Revival Hubs and Church Models.....17

4. Dry Bones and New Wineskins.....27

5. Intercession: The Foundation of Every Revival Hub.....35

6. Prophetic Worship: Releasing the Sound of Awakening.....49

7. Forging Revival Tribes.....59

8. Pressing Into the Supernatural.....67

9. Engaging Principalities and Powers.....77

10. Team Ministry That Releases Synergies.....85

11. Digging Wells and Building Walls.....101

12. Shifting Spiritual Climates.....109

13. Revival Zones: Transforming and Reforming Cities
    and Regions.....121

14. A Nehemiah Company of Revival Hub Builders
    on the Wall.....131

15. Laying the Foundation for Generational Revival.....141

FOREWORD

January 13, 1991 was a rewarding day for the congregation and staff of Brownsville Assembly of God in Pensacola, Florida. It had been an arduous three-year journey; but the new sanctuary was completed, and dedication Sunday had finally arrived. We had planned, given freely and prepared extensively for this event. The church grew on that first Sunday, gaining 600 new attendees immediately. Our attendance jumped from 1,000 to 1600, and we never turned back.

The week of dedication happened during the First Gulf War in Iraq under President George H. W. Bush. There was such sensitivity to the signs of the times that America's churches were filled nationwide. Curiosity concerning the new building, the outbreak of war and a fresh move of God's Spirit at Brownsville, put us in a very good position as a church. Long awaited success had finally come.

Shortly thereafter, on a Saturday, I went to the church to pray. Before I locked myself in the building, I looked around to make sure the sanctuary was empty. I did not want anyone to hear me pour my heart out to God.

My prayer started out as an apology to the Lord. I said, "Lord, I am so blessed to be the husband of such a godly and loving wife and to be the father of two outstanding sons that have never given me a moment of trouble. I am on television worldwide, and I pastor a great congregation in a great city; but Lord, I feel so lonely…I hurt…I feel so empty. Why do I ache in my soul?"

Immediately, I heard Holy Spirit me say within, "If you will return to the God of your childhood, I will touch you afresh and anew." Then the Lord said to me, "If you will make this house a house of prayer, I will pour out my Spirit in this place in a mighty way that will astound you!"

This resonated powerfully in my spirit. I knew I had to make Brownsville a house of prayer. However, I also knew that prayer meetings could be the least attended gatherings at many churches. I was literally sweating the prospect of trying to rally the troops for persistent congregational prayer; but the Lord said to me, "I will give you the plan." He did, and it was a concise plan.

As we began to pray, it felt as though revival would break out any moment. However, as we continued to pray, and the weeks turned into months, and the months to years, it seemed that revival would never happen. I learned quickly that if you are praying about something and it seems like it is about to happen, it probably is not. However, if you have prayed, and prayed, and it seems it will never happen, it is probably right at the door. Although we were weary in well doing, we would not quit. We prayed two and one-half years for revival.

Someone once said that sometimes prayer is like digging holes; and at other times, prayer is like planting poles. There are times that prayer is like stretching wire, but then there are times it is like pulling the lever; and CONTACT, the power flows!

On Father's Day 1995, the fumes of two and one-half years of intercessory prayer, repentance and warfare were in the sanctuary. Evangelist Steve Hill became the match that God used to ignite those fumes—revival exploded! It was so powerful in my life that I had an epiphany. From that moment on, I referred to my ministry as B.R. (Before Revival) and A.R. (After Revival).

Time will not permit me to elaborate on many of the important details of the revival, which became known by many names, such as the Pensacola Outpouring, the Father's Day Outpouring and the Brownsville Revival. This move of the Spirit brought 4.5 million hungry souls from the nations of the earth into a small town in West Florida to have a rendezvous with the fire of God.

I have often said that once you have had your feet under the table of Holy Ghost revival, no other table will ever satisfy your soul. I could never return to normal church again. That is why I am honored to write the introduction to "Revival Hubs Rising." As I read the manuscript, I could not help but breathe a sigh of relief because someone finally has gotten it right. Jennifer LeClaire and Ryan LeStrange have masterfully envisioned the next great move of God.

We are living in the most intriguing times the Church has ever known. The Church is changing, and it is changing quickly. I have never known a time when God's people are dreaming as they are dreaming. People are having visions. Worship is at new level. The Church is opening up to the five-fold ministry as never before. The last days of this dispensation are no longer coming; they are here now. All the dynamics are in motion to experience a nationwide and worldwide revival.

When I saw the Twin Towers fall on September 11, 2001, I cried out to the Lord and asked if this meant revival was over. The Lord responded quickly, but firmly, in my spirit. He said, "No, I will pour out My Spirit, and revival will break forth again; but it will be in conjunction with end of the age events and the fulfillment of the signs of My soon coming." Ladies and gentlemen, we are now at that juncture. I am so encouraged that even though there are signs—serious signs—happening in our world almost daily, I know that revival does not happen in the best of times. Revival usually breaks forth in the worst of times.

The purpose of this book is to shift our thinking and lift our vision from a localized church revival, to revival hotspots that will fervently burn throughout our nation and world until our Lord returns. The wineskins are already filling up with fresh ideas, prophetic worship, supernatural cravings for signs following those that minister, and last but not least, the reality of His house truly becoming a house of prayer among all nations.

I am convinced much work has already been done, and the lever is about to be pulled. The revival hubs are about to light up! It is only a matter of time.

John A. Kilpatrick
Founder and Senior Pastor
Church of His Presence
Daphne, Alabama

1

REVIVAL HUBS RISING

Revival hubs. Apostolic centers. Houses of prayer. Kingdom centers. Glory hubs. There are many different ways to describe the emerging model of church-as-we-have-never-known-it, but all of them break the traditional Sunday morning mold—and they all have at least one thing in common: they are rising up out of intercession from hearts desperate for more of God.

For the sake of our study—and given the many prophetic words about revival and awakening in America and the nations of the earth—we'll use the term revival hubs. (We'll define these hubs in greater detail in the next chapter.) But no matter what you call them, God is speaking to many in His body about a new "church" wineskin in this hour.

We've both received prophetic words about how the Holy Spirit wants to raise up and work through revival hubs and we've talked to a number of revivalists who have heard similar things in their spirit. We believe thousands of believers across the United States and around the world are sensing the rise of these revival hubs but don't necessarily have language to describe it. We believe that because people have told us.

In this chapter, we'll share a few prophetic words and insights to prime the pump of your faith and light a fire in your heart. It is our hope that these prophetic words and definitions will give you some common language so communicating about what God is doing will be easier.

AN ERUPTING VISION OF REVIVAL HUBS

Ryan was in prayer seeking God about His plans for the nations when suddenly a vision erupted in his spirit. He saw light springing forth from various places in the world. The following goes into detail about the vision.

I began to ask the Lord: What am I seeing? He spoke to me that these are global revival hubs. Each hub is a strategic place of outpouring. As the Lord continued to reveal to me His plans for revival centers and hubs He showed me that they would function differently than what I would typically perceive as a revival center.

The hubs are not only called to be places of revival and outpouring but also of equipping and advancing. Radical moves of the Spirit and hosting the presence of God are only part of the call of these emerging centers. These must also be places that teach, activate and equip the body of Christ for Last Days harvest and every member must be active.

I see a great wave of glory coming upon the hubs! The hubs will carry different expressions of revival in this hour yet each is vital to the Father's plans. We must be cautious not to attempt to create a cookie-cutter pattern for the revival centers and hubs that God is establishing. I heard the Lord say:

"This is the discovery of a paradigm that will unleash a global harvest as My plans and purposes are fulfilled in the earth. I'm building

the foundation for revival and revival centers, it is not the work of man but the ordination of my spirit."

THIS IS NOT A NEW MODEL AT ALL

Of course, what the Lord wants to do in this hour is not really a new thing. We know that there's nothing new under the sun (see Ecclesiastes 1:9). As you read through this book, you'll see time and time again how God is restoring the original blueprint of the church. The Holy Spirit spoke these words to Jennifer about revival hubs:

"I am raising up a new model, which is not a new model at all. I am causing revival-minded believers to return to the Book of Acts and giving them revelation on the original model of My Church.

"This model is a new wineskin in which I will pour out My Spirit. This model will sustain My glory because it will steward My presence. This model will focus on equipping and sending rather than gathering and grooming. This model will establish leaders, mature intercessors, and make an impact on the cities and regions in which they are established. This model will manifest both the apostolic and the prophetic and rely on five-fold gifts working in unison to advance the Kingdom.

"This model will be rejected and despised by the religious leaders of the day but make no mistake: I am working in this model. I am restoring the church to its original model. I am coming back for a church without spot or wrinkle and that means cleaning up the structure and truly preparing the Bride for Christ's return.

"Those who truly embrace this model will feel the wind of My Spirit blowing over them, My favor resting upon them, My grace empowering them, and My anointing to set the captives free and bring lost souls into the kingdom within them. It's all in the Book of Acts, a book which has no end because you are living in it. Seek My model."

This is a powerful prophetic word that should cause us to reexamine how we do church. Think about it for a minute. When revival comes, it's going to change church as usual. Traditional churches will have to focus more on discipleship because of all the new converts. Teachers will need to rise up. We'll need more pastors. Revival hubs are not suited for a one-man paradigm—and the religious spirit that longs to be seen of men will hate that.

A Prophetic Key Putting Revival Hubs on the Map

Revival hubs are emerging—but it's going to require the apostolic and prophetic working together to fully establish this new wine skin. Essentially, it's the same principle as establishing a traditional church, though most traditional churches do not follow this principle. Most traditional churches are still building on the five-fold gift of the pastor and many reject the notion that God has restored apostolic and prophetic ministry.

Paul the apostle explained in Ephesians 2:20-22: "Having been built upon the foundation of the apostles and prophets, Jesus Christ Himself being the chief cornerstone, in whom the entire building, tightly framed together, grows into a holy temple in the Lord, in whom you also are being built together into a dwelling place of God through the Spirit."

This is one of the goals of a revival center.

James Goll, president of Encounters Network, director of Prayer Storm, and coordinator of Encounter Alliance, a coalition of leaders, had a clear vision of how the apostolic and prophetic would work together in establishing what he calls apostolic renewal centers, which is one more way to describe revival hubs.

In Harrisburg, Pennsylvania, Goll saw, written out before his eyes, the letters A, M and P. He watched it and the "M" moved in front of the "A" and then spelled MAP. AMP and MAP. He asked God "What is this?" He says God told him, "When the apostolic 'A' is made 'P' personal"—and Goll says the word "personal" is really important—"I will put those apostolic renewal centers on my MAP."

The following is the prophetic word Goll shared:

"I will amplify my voice and I will put them on My MAP. When the apostolic is made personal, there will be Mighty authority in the prophetic in that place. I will amplify my voice, and I will put those apostolic renewal centers on my map. It's not primarily structural—it's primarily relational."

Goll explains that when the apostolic is made personal there will be mighty authority in the prophetic because prophetic people will be secure and will move out and God will amplify His voice. People are drawn to the voice of the Lord, and He will put those places on His map. They won't have to put something big in a magazine. God will put them on His map, and people will come. If He builds, it they will come.

The prophetic word continues:

"So many times My people have erred because they have built a structure for themselves to fill, and then I have to tear down the very structures that I even called them to. And I have to oppose that of which they began to do in the Spirit. For have you not read in the book of Galatians, 'Oh you foolish Galatians, who has bewitched you? You who began in the Spirit, do you believe that you can be perfected by the works of the flesh?

I am raising up an abandoned remnant of people, and they shall not put structure as their foremost emphasis but they will rather put "I Am"—the Architect. "I Am. I Am." The "I Am" is the architect. For

Abraham went forth looking for a builder. For many men and women are going to cemeteries to go learn how things are laid out neatly and in order, and everything is dead there. It is all laid out neatly and in order. But I am now calling forth the people that will look for the Architect that lives in heaven. I will raise up many authentic, apostolic renewal/ revival centers in the earth."

GLORY HUBS AND TRANSFORMATION CENTERS

Chuck Pierce, founder of Glory of Zion Ministries, in 2014 convened a national consultation of apostolic centers called Apostolic Centers Rising. "The Lord is creating a new model for gathering," says Pierce. "This includes community interaction as well as tabernacle worship. Apostolic centers are arising throughout the earth. These will become glory hubs for the next move of God. They will also become known as transformation centers." Pierce also uses the name "freedom posts" to describe the emerging revival hubs.

"He showed me that His remnant was building new freedom outposts or apostolic centers. He called this remnant His 'triumphant reserve.' I saw 23 freedom outposts in 23 states. He then showed me other outposts that needed to form in some places, and still others where the spiritual atmosphere was now not conducive to freedom," says Pierce.

"Since 2009, the Lord has been developing and identifying apostolic centers for the future. These centers will be used to produce a threefold generational Kingdom advancement. By 2016 there would have to be a revolution of revelation attached to the apostolic centers. These centers, or outposts, will be known as contending governmental influences very much like in John the Baptist, Jesus, and the apostles' day. Once again, the Lord's warning to 'beware of the Pharisees and Herodians' will become a reality! The covenant rights of this land will once again be contended for."

THE TWELVE CITY PROPHECY

In 1989, Rick Joyner, founder of MorningStar Ministries and author of books like *I See a New America*, saw 12 cities in which revival would break out. He published this vision in the *MorningStar Journal* 1992 and called it "The Twelve City Prophecy." It was published in Volume 2, No. 3 originally and later published in Volume 11, No. 1 in case you want to order a copy of the entire vision.

"In the vision, I saw circles drawn around each of these cities that I later estimated to be about 1,000 miles in diameter or to have a radius of 500 miles," he wrote. "I then estimated that over 98% of the population of the US was within 500 miles of at least one of these cities or a one-day drive. These cities are strategically located according to the population centers."

The cities Joyner saw in his vision were: Albany, New York; Atlanta; Columbus, OH, Dallas-Fort-Worth, Denver, Kansas City, Minneapolis-St. Paul, Orlando, Phoenix, Portland, Santa Maria, California and Washington, D.C. Could it be possible that these cities will be home to strategic revival hubs in the days ahead?

In the next chapter, we'll dive deeper into the concept of revival hubs, as well as exploring specific characteristics that help define them.

2

WHAT IS A REVIVAL HUB?

What is a revival hub? That's a question many are asking in this hour as God breathes on this ministry model. As we mentioned in chapter one, revival hubs are emerging and evolving and take on different flavors—and not everyone uses the term revival hub. Again, some call them apostolic centers, houses of prayer, missions bases, kingdom centers, glory hubs and so on.

Although you don't see the term revival hub in the Bible, it's a new wineskin—or perhaps better called a resurrection of the original model of church—that is clearly presented in the Book of Acts. Here is our definition of a revival hub: a center that is focused on digging and maintaining a rich well of revival and Spirit-led ministry unto equipping, awakening and societal transformation. A revival hub is a base of tactical operation, organization, and deployment.

Father is placing men and women in small towns and big cities to dig deep wells of revival and refreshing. He is establishing ministries that will, when they mature, serve as a hub of awakening in their region, where people come and go to get refreshed and equipped. Radical revivalists whose heart cry is to see a Third Great Awakening will steward divine outpourings in revival hubs. The vision is not merely to build a ministry that blesses people but to release the spiritual destiny of a city or region, host the presence of God, and facilitate a radical transformation in hearts and minds that ultimately changes the spiritual climate.

Think about it for a minute. What would it look like if a group of people gathered in unity and holiness to cry out to the Lord? What would it look like if people in your region began to share the gospel with signs and wonders following? What would it look like if the church in your region was alive and fully awake to the spirit realm? What would it look like if God was encountering people in your region and drawing them to salvation? We submit to you that it would look much different than it does now. But what does a revival hub look like? We'll compare and contrast emerging revival hubs with traditional church, but first, let's look at some other paradigms.

New Wineskins Emerging

We gave you our definition of a revival hub: a center that is focused on digging and maintaining a rich well of revival and Spirit-led ministry unto equipping, awakening and societal transformation. There are other names for essentially the same model, and some focus more on worship and prayer while others focus more on leadership training and equipping. Before we move on to look at the key characteristics of revival hubs, let's look at some of the other paradigms that are essentially revival hubs by another name. The key difference is the revival hub is focused more on revival and awakening than some these other models. But they are all new wineskins.

Let's start with houses of prayer. We believe the house of prayer movement was a forerunner for revival hubs. After all, revival hubs are birthed out of intercession—and intercession is a key component of revival hubs. My (Jennifer) revival hub in Hollywood, FL morphed from a house of prayer. We started with intercession. Then we added the missions base component. The missions base combines prayer with works of service and has an equipping component. IHOPKC is a strong example of a missions base. Full-time staff at IHOPKC are known as "intercessory missionaries" who raise their own support to do the work of the Lord. IHOPKC describes itself with this language:

"The International House of Prayer is an evangelical missions organization that is committed to praying for the release of the fullness of God's power and purpose, as we actively win the lost, heal the sick, feed the poor, make disciples, and impact every sphere of society—family, education, government, economy, arts, media, religion, etc. Our vision is to work in relationship with the wider Body of Christ to engage in the Great Commission, as we seek to walk out the two great commandments to love God and people." IHOPKC is one of the largest revival hubs in America.

Apostolic centers have emerged in church vocabulary as the apostolic movement has matured. Dr. C. Peter Wagner launched a network of leaders who started a movement of apostolic centers in the United States and around the world. Apostolic centers are built on the first century church model and are working to change the way we look at modern church. An apostolic center is heavy on equipping, mobilizing, and sending into kingdom works.

"The modus operandi of the first century church was as follows: an apostle would found a congregation, stay long enough to nurture elders, and then the apostle would leave that city to found another citywide movement of congregations but continue to revisit each of these churches and give them guidance and oversee them, but of course from a macro level," says Joseph Mattera, presiding bishop of Christ Covenant Coalition, overseeing bishop of Resurrection Church in New York, and U.S. ambassador for the International Coalition of Apostles. "They use the term 'centers' rather than churches perhaps to disassociate themselves from the baggage of the present day church."

Kingdom centers are an evolution or expression of apostolic centers but have an intentional blueprint. Ken Malone, founder of Forerunner Ministries, expresses a model that includes a command center, prayer center, training center, healing center and apostolic network. "Church is who we are—not just where we assemble on Sunday," Malone says. "The church has been given the keys to steward the kingdom of God in the earth and unlock His plans in the earth."

Greg Crawford, founder of The Base Iowa, defines a kingdom center as a stewardship center that serves a region. As he explains it, it has a visionary apostolic leader appointed as oversight, not of people, but gifting in people: "Along with prophetic gifting and insights, a team ministry is formed that actually becomes a stewardship center of how God is forming the Kingdom over a region. They train to release the hidden potential they see, and implement plans to mobilize those of like faith to accomplish Kingdom mandates."

Chuck Pierce, founder of Glory of Zion Ministries, talks of apostolic centers, freedom outposts and glory hubs. Some of these terms are somewhat interchangeable yet also distinctive in terms of how God is moving in a region. A glory hub, for example, may be revival-minded but is marked by the notable glory of God. Bethel, for example, is a missions base with a clear revival mandate that may be best be described as a glory hub. Glory clouds literally roll through Bethel Redding—and signs and wonders are normal occurrences. As you can see, a new wineskin has emerged with different expressions. Revival hubs are rising rapidly.

KEY CHARACTERISTICS OF REVIVAL HUBS

God is releasing a vision for revival and awakening to many believers in various streams in the body of Christ. Revival hubs are marked by presence-driven people and are home to healing wells. Revival hubs are soul-saving stations and places of supernatural deliverance and restoration. Revival hubs are equipping centers, a place of family, strategy, apostolic ministry and prophetic identity.

We'll compare revival hubs and church models in Chapter 3, but let's drill into some more earmarks of revival hubs to lay a foundation before we get there. A revival hub is a place of continued refreshing and outpouring as opposed to a place that enjoys a seasonal outpouring. This is an expression of the apostolic mandate to build places of presence and power. Revival hubs are also places of prayer and intimacy that are marked by hunger—the hungry will press in and invite an outpouring in a region. Revival hubs dwellers are well diggers. They dig wells that will not only bless the revival hub but help transform a region.

"Revival hubs are filled with people who have great expectancy and hunger for God—they are ready for more of Him," says Joe Joe Dawson, president of Burn Texarkana, a revival hub and house of prayer, and a leader in the New Breed Revival Network. "There is an increasing amount of the power and presence of God in revival hubs. The glory is there and it draws people in."

Revival hubs release the sounds of heaven, which we'll discuss more in Chapter 6. For now, we'll just say that prophetic worship marks revival hubs. God is birthing new sounds for a new move.

There is no room for performance-driven worship in revival hubs. The worship that is coming forth draws people deeper into powerful encounters with Jesus. Revival hubs are known for miracles and power. They are centers of supernatural power where bodies are healed, live changed and miracles released.

Revival hubs embrace the full five-fold ministry. They are places of fathering, imparting, activating and sending. God is raising up revival hubs that are birthing and establishing spiritual sons and daughters. As the move of God continues, training is key to raise up a generation that releases the Kingdom. Team ministry and leadership models mark revival hubs. They carry an apostolic structure rather than a political structure. Revival hubs will face opposition as the well runs deeper and the transforming presence of God grows—but revival hub dwellers will not shrink back.

Of course, no two revival hubs look exactly alike. Revival hubs will take on different structures and flows depending on the leadership team's mandate and giftings. For example, some revival hubs will carry a strong apostolic spirit while others may serve as more of a prayer base and still others will put a heavier emphasis on training. That said, mature revival hubs will carry a full representation of the five ministry gifts—apostolic, prophetic, evangelistic, pastoral and teaching. Mature revival hubs, then, will have a multiplicity of ministry and will equip the people to dig the wells of revival in the territory.

By the same token, some revival hubs will have a very active local church ministry, gathering people for weekly training, equipping and fellowship. Others will have a broader regional focus and remain outside of the church wineskin, networking with churches from many streams and functioning as a training center with a revival-mandate.

AN EQUIPPING MANDATE

We mentioned the equipping aspect but it's worth re-emphasizing. Revival hubs carry a mandate for regional equipping, impartation and activation that leads to and sustains revival unto awakening unto transformation unto reformation. Revival hubs are called to embrace partnership between the apostolic and prophetic. The apostolic anointing is a building and governing anointing while the prophetic anointing is a revelation and warfare anointing.

In healthy, Christ-centered revival hubs, apostolic and prophetic gifts, along with Jesus as the Chief Cornerstone, lay the foundation (see Ephesians 2:20). But revival hubs are not about apostles and prophets alone. Revival hubs thrive when all five ministry gifts are functioning in their proper order to equip the saints for the work of the ministry. Let's take a closer look at that concept.

"He gave some to be apostles, prophets, evangelists, pastors, and teachers, for the equipping of the saints, for the work of service, and for the building up of the body of Christ, until we all come into the unity of the faith and of the knowledge of the Son of God, into a complete man, to the measure of the stature of the fullness of Christ, so we may no longer be children, tossed here and there by waves and carried about with every wind of doctrine by the trickery of men, by craftiness with deceitful scheming. But, speaking the truth in love, we may grow up in all things into Him, who is the head, Christ Himself, from whom the whole body is joined together and connected by every joint and ligament, as every part effectively does its work and grows, building itself up in love" (Ephesians 4:11-16).

While Paul traveled as an apostolic missionary, planting and building revival hubs in the midst of what was the greatest spiritual awakening the world has ever seen after the first coming, death and resurrection of Christ, he had this equipping mandate in mind. Healthy revival centers are not based on a one-man paradigm but value every gift and equip every saint that has a heart to make an impact in their sphere of influence. Our friend Chris Mathis, lead pastor at The Summit in Crestview, Florida and a leader in the New Breed Revival Network, puts it this way: "Revival hubs are places that ministers get sent out and get sent in. There is a constant flow in and out for the Kingdom to advance."

In the next chapter, we'll learn more about what revival hubs are—and what they are not—by comparing and contrasting revival hubs with the traditional church model.

3

COMPARING REVIVAL HUBS
AND CHURCH MODELS

Revival hubs break the mold of traditional churches. Dutch Sheets, a best-selling author and international speaker, once said, "I don't want to pastor a local church. God is calling me to lead an apostolic center for kingdom ministry."

Although they may not use terms like apostolic center, kingdom ministry or even revival hubs, many pastors we talk to feel the same. They know there's something more. They sense God moving in a new way and they long for the fresh wind of the Spirit to blow over their ministry.

In fact, many pastors are burning out on church as usual. According to a *New York Times* report, "Members of the clergy now suffer from obesity, hypertension and depression at rates higher than most Americans. In the past decade, their use of antidepressants has risen while their life expectancy has fallen. Many would change jobs if they could." George Barna's *Today's Pastors* reveals 53 percent of pastors believe the church is showing little positive impact on the world around them and 60 percent believe that church ministry has negatively impacted their passion for church work. Only 4 percent of senior pastors have a clear vision for their church.

In 2012, Chuck Pierce, founder of Glory of Zion Ministries, declared, "This is a time to break out of the shell of our last identity, whether good or bad. God is doing a new thing with His people and creating a new model of kingdom authority on earth."

See, there's local church life and then there's Kingdom life. Many times, we're so focused on church that we miss the Kingdom. Revival hubs produce believers that seek first the Kingdom of God and His righteousness, and then everything else falls into place (see Matthew 6:33). Now that we have a baseline foundation for what a revival hub is, we can gain a deeper understanding by comparing and contrasting revival hubs with traditional churches.

A REFRESHING KINGDOM PARADIGM

The story of Jairus' daughter in Mark 5 offers a significant prophetic message for the church in this hour. Doubtless, you are familiar with the story but let's look at it through a prophetic lens:

"One of the rulers of the synagogue, named Jairus, saw Jesus and came and fell at His feet and earnestly asked Him, "My little daughter is lying at the point of death. I ask You, come and lay Your hands on her, so that she may be healed. And she will live." So Jesus went with him. And many people followed Him and pressed in on Him" (Mark 5:22-24).

Now, Jairus was a religious ruler of the day—in fact, he was a ruler of the synagogue in Capernaum—yet he was coming to this controversial "prophet" pleading for the life of his ailing daughter. Let's stop right there for a minute. A ruler of a synagogue was "an official appointed by the elders to look after the building, its contents, and its arrangements for worship," according to *Oxford Bible Studies*. Sounds sort of like a pastor.

Jairus was unique among religious leaders of his day. Remember, most of the Pharisees and Sadducees argued with and falsely accused Jesus. Some even suggested He had a devil. Another ruler of a synagogue we see in Scripture got bent out of shape because Jesus healed on the Sabbath (see Luke 13:14). Jairus' willingness to move outside his religious box is something from which we can all learn.

Indeed, Jairus boldness to embrace a new paradigm of the Kingdom gives us a glimpse into the heart of revival hubs and their leaders. See, there is a holy pleading that takes places for a people, a region—a nation! A revival hub is a place dedicated to personal and corporate revival and awakening. It is a place that gears its entire ministry around the purpose of revival, which includes reaching the lost and equipping the saints.

Jairus not only sought the manifest power of God but also put a value on the presence of God. He wanted Jesus to come to his house. He invited the King into his dwelling place. Revival hubs dig deep wells of divine encounter and presence. Revival hub leaders are committed to hosting the presence of God on both a personal and corporate level. But there is more to this revelation.

WAKING UP THE SLEEPING CHURCH

"He came to the house of the ruler of the synagogue, and saw the tumult, and those who wept and wailed loudly. When He came in, He said to them, "Why make this uproar and weep? The girl is not dead, but sleeping." They laughed at Him in ridicule. But when He had put them all out, He took the father and the mother of the girl and those who were with Him and entered where the girl was lying.

He took the girl by the hand and said to her, *"Talitha cumi,"* which means, "Little girl, I say to you, arise." Immediately the girl arose and walked, for she was twelve years of age. And they were greatly astonished. He strictly ordered them to let no one know of it and directed them to give her something to eat" (Mark 5:38-43).

From a natural perspective, Jairus' daughter was dead. But Jesus looked beyond the natural into another dimension—the spirit realm—and saw life. Then, He boldly declared what He saw. It seemed absolutely absurd! In the same way, the Holy Spirit is releasing vision into regions and territories that seem utterly ridiculous to traditional thinkers. He is releasing a spirit of bravery and boldness to look far beyond the present natural condition and lay claim to the unseen promises—even to the impossible unto the miraculous.

The enemy delivered a deathblow to this 12-year-old girl. Twelve is a number that holds fascinating biblical meaning: completeness, perfection and authority. There were 12 tribes in Israel. Jesus chose 12 disciples. The New Jerusalem that descends out of heaven has 12 gates made of pearl, manned by 12 angels.

We believe the church (the ekklessia) is moving into a place of greater completion, maturity and authority. We are transitioning from an old wineskin to a new one. We are moving from tradition to travail, from placating to proclaiming, from maintaining to multiplying and from entertaining to equipping! There is a bold prophetic call going forth to arise and build the revival hubs! To some, it may seem ridiculous. To others, it may sound crazy. Nevertheless, we must break free from the fear of man to enter into this new Kingdom paradigm.

Imagine how radical it was for Jesus to encounter a grieving family staring at a cold body and boldly proclaim that she was not dead—

and then kick them out of the room! Most Bible-believing Christians would be outraged. But the results of this radical proclamation speak for themselves: the daughter rose from the dead. Now consider this: Jairus' daughter represents the sleeping church. We are believing for the same miracle in this day: an awakened and alive church full of power, purpose and glory.

REVIVAL HUB LEADERS ARE CALLED, MANDATED AND MANTLED

We defined revival hubs in Chapter 2. The very definition displays some of the differences between traditional churches and revival hubs. But let's go deeper and get understanding on the wisdom the Holy Spirit is pouring out in this hour. Let's explore how hubs look and function compared to the traditional church model.

This is an important discussion because fear can cause good people who love God with pure passion to reject the unknown. It is critical that we understand God is raising up revival hubs to partner with and strengthen the body of Christ—not to compete with or tear down local assemblies. Sure, there are always some rebellious or wounded believers in the body who will grab any and every new teaching or revelation to justify rebellion against the church. But revival hubs are not born out of rebellion. Revival hubs are birthed out of a passion for transforming revival.

Revival hubs begin with a divine call to a region or people. There is a moment of revelation like Moses experienced at the burning bush—a moment of divine calling. I (Ryan) met a media leader who had been involved in ministry for over 20 years—and who loved the Lord with all his heart, was active in ministry, and studied his Bible daily—knew something was missing. In prayer, the Holy Spirit told him it was time to go deeper.

At that moment, he received two calls: (1) to love God and pursue Him on a deeper level through radical worship and (2) to become a media revivalist and host a revival hub. As he cooperated with the Holy Spirit everything changed! His personal prayer life changed. His relationship with Holy Spirit intensified and advanced. The flow of his ministry and his media production shifted. God's glory began to radiate in his media revival hub. Miracles and healing poured out rivers of living water.

Every revival hub begins with a call and a mandate. We see this in Scripture over and over again, from Moses to Isaiah to Gideon to Jeremiah to the disciples of Christ, to Paul the apostle and beyond. Let's take a look at one example from Exodus 3:2-10:

"The angel of the Lord appeared to him in a flame of fire from the midst of a bush, and he looked, and the bush burned with fire, but the bush was not consumed. So Moses said, 'I will now turn aside and see this great sight, why the bush is not burnt.' When the Lord saw that he turned aside to see, God called to him from out of the midst of the bush and said, "Moses, Moses. "And he said, 'Here am I.'"

"He said, 'Do not approach here. Remove your sandals from off your feet, for the place on which you are standing is holy ground.' Moreover He said, 'I am the God of your father, the God of Abraham, the God of Isaac, and the God of Jacob.' And Moses hid his face, for he was afraid to look upon God.

"The Lord said, 'I have surely seen the affliction of My people who are in Egypt and have heard their cry on account of their taskmasters, for I know their sorrows. Therefore, I have come down to deliver them out of the hand of the Egyptians, and to bring them up out of that land to a good and spacious land, to a land flowing with milk and honey, to the place of the Canaanites, the Hittites, the Amorites, the Perizzites, the Hivites, and the Jebusites.

Now therefore, the cry of the children of Israel has come to Me. Moreover, I have also seen the oppression with which the Egyptians are oppressing them. Come now therefore, and I will send you to Pharaoh so that you may bring forth My people, the children of Israel, out of Egypt."

Again, every revival hub begins with a mandate. The Lord visits a person or a group much like He visited Moses and releases a call to dig a well. There is a divine discovery of a regional mandate. Remember these words the Lord spoke to Jeremiah: "Seek the peace of the city where I have caused you to be carried away captive, and pray to the Lord for it; for in its peace you will have peace" (Jeremiah 29:7). God is releasing mantles in this hour to revivalists who will press into what He is calling them to do in their city and region.

COMPARING AND CONTRASTING CHURCHES AND HUBS

The following is a comparison between emerging revival hubs and the traditional church. This is in no way meant to disparage the church. We love the church. God is leading many of His people to embrace a new wineskin, which we'll talk about in the next chapter. The next points aim to show you how this new wineskin differs from the old.

- Revival hubs focus on hosting glory of God and a regional purpose. Traditional churches are focused on ministering to the felt needs of a people or community.
- Revival hubs dig a well of revival and fosters Holy Ghost power-based ministry with signs, wonders and miracles. Traditional churches birth and create programs to address

the needs of the people.

- Revival hubs make transformation the central focus, which means change and willingness to be uncomfortable. Traditional churches make growth and attendance the central focus—"keep the people comfortable so they will keep coming."

- Revival hubs challenge the culture, engage in spiritual warfare, and blast the ruling spirits and strongholds that have been established in a region. Traditional churches work to be culturally relevant and add cultural norms into the flavor of the ministry.

- Revival hubs build on a foundation of prayer, take the house of prayer mission seriously, and will sacrifice plans, resources and programs for prayer. Traditional churches may have a weekly prayer meeting but typically do not view corporate prayer and intercession as a primary mandate.

- Revival hubs partner with diverse voices and gifts in the body of Christ, bringing them into the territory to make a spiritual deposit. Traditional churches build on the "senior pastor" gift and may have guests occasionally that preach along similar lines.

- Revival hubs are a place of His presence, and make the presence of God the aim of success for corporate gatherings. Traditional churches enjoy the presence of God but may be afraid of the Holy Spirit's intensity or radical outpourings that offend some people and impact attendance and giving.

- Revival hubs value the five ministry gifts and embrace a team ministry concept. This can manifest in multiple ways: in-house teams, long distance teams, cooperative partnerships and ministry relationships. Traditional churches are comfortable with leaders and positions but everything is governed through a pastor and church model that does not necessarily embrace five-fold ministry of the concept of a fully functioning team.

- Revival hubs are equipping centers. These are not just a place to receive healing or prophecy but a place to be equipped to heal the sick and minister prophetically. While there are radical moves of God's Spirit to release gifts, there is also a strong focus on depositing and activating gifts. Revival hubs move from teaching to mentoring and fathering. Traditional churches are primarily a teaching center, communicating concepts, tools and principles for living without actually training and activating the saints for the work of the ministry (see Ephesians 4:11-13).

- Revival hubs move, advance and evolve—the apostolic spirit is in constant motion. Apostolic people must progress, grow and change because revival is a continual journey. A revival hub is a place of advancement with leaders who are not afraid to receive new light, revelation or instruction. Traditional churches build a safe, comfortable place, value continuity and tradition, do not want to rock the boat or make people nervous, and cling to familiarity as a sign of spirituality.

- Revival hubs train, release and send, network, impart and impact. Traditional churches gather, grow, maintain, teach, and meet needs and comfort.

- Revival hubs release new sounds. Traditional churches sing familiar songs.

- Revival hubs bring the prayer room into the main room,

build prayer-based worship ministry that pioneers prophetic worship and values spontaneity. Traditional churches gather "the best" local musicians to sing everyone's favorite songs.

- Revival hub congregants heal the sick, open healing ministries, press in and believe for miracles, activate and awaken the supernatural in a region, and become a voice of healing in the land. Traditional churches may pray for the sick but typically do not equip people to heal the sick through team ministry; these churches are careful not to believe too big due to fear of failure.

- Revival hub leaders not only make room for a move of the Spirit but also teach and explain the "whys and hows" of spiritual principles and outpourings. Revival hubs become a leading voice of revival in a territory. Traditional churches teach the people of God to love God and may move in the Spirit but do not typically train believers to operate in the gifts or establish a strong voice of cultural transformation in a region.

- Revival hubs are governing ministries in a region; governing in prayer, the Word (prevailing teaching); in vision; and in authority (power). Traditional churches typically are focused on building a successful ministry filled with people.

Can you see the differences? We're not at all against the local church, nor is it the intent of revival hubs to "steal sheep" from local congregations. Many people come to my (Jennifer) revival hub on Sunday afternoon's after their traditional church to get equipped and take what they learned back to their home church.

In the next chapter, we'll explore dry bones and new wineskins.

4

Dry Bones and New Wineskins

We both love the church with a passion, but the sad reality is some churches are lukewarm instead of on fire for God. Other churches have quenched the Holy Spirit. Still other churches don't believe the gifts of the Spirit are for today. People often tell us their churches are dry or feel spiritually dead. There are no signs, no wonders, no miracles—no spiritual gifts or rivers of living water flowing. Yet in the Book of Acts we see signs, wonders, miracles and flowing spiritual gifts as normal Christianity.

What has happened? In some cases, religion has crept in. In other cases, there is sin in church leadership and the Holy Spirit won't move until repentance comes. In still other churches, people just don't know what they don't know. In other words, they've just been doing church the way it was handed down to them, from generation to generation. Here's a sad statement from a Third-World believer: "It is amazing what the church in the West has been able to achieve without the Holy Spirit."

What an indictment! It's time to pour the water of the Spirit over the dry bones. See, bones deal with structure and foundations. God wants to breathe new life on the foundations of church structure.

You've probably heard prophets—forerunners—lifting their voices with words of reformation over the body of Christ. Here's what we know: as the wind comes upon the dry bones, a mighty army is released. God wants to raise up a mighty army in the nations of the earth in this hour, led forth by the Captain of the Hosts.

Contending in the Valley of Dry Bones

It's a process—and revival hubs embrace the process. Let's look at the process. We'll find it in Ezekiel 37. Ezekiel, a priest, prophet and watchman who had extraordinary visions, stood in the Valley of Dry Bones.

"The hand of the Lord was upon me, and He carried me out in the Spirit of the Lord and set me down in the midst of the valley which was full of bones, and He caused me to pass among them all around. And there were very many in the open valley. And they were very dry" (Ezekiel 37:1-3).

Imagine this scene. The bones weren't just dry—they were "very dry." There weren't just a few bones lying around. The valley was full of bones. In this hour, much of the church finds itself in the valley instead of on the mountaintop, persecuted by antichrist agendas and unsure how to respond—or too fearful to respond at all.

Like Ezekiel, the Lord is asking us a question, "Can these bones live?" (Ezekiel 37:3). Many are responding just like Ezekiel did, uncertain if it's too late for their church, their city, or their nation. They are answering, "O Lord God, You know" (Ezekiel 37:3). Let's listen in to what happens next:

"Again He said to me, 'Prophesy over these bones and say to them, O dry bones, hear the word of the Lord. Thus says the Lord God to these bones: I will cause breath to enter you so that you live.

And I will lay sinews upon you and will grow back flesh upon you and cover you with skin and put breath in you so that you live. Then you shall know that I am the Lord" (Ezekiel 37:4-6).

In this hour, when so much of the church is lukewarm, dry—or even apostate—we need to rise up and prophesy God's will instead of tapping into the doom, gloom, curses judgments that leave no room for the mercy of God. Jesus is in the restoration business. He is in the resurrection business. He is in the transformation business. We need to prophesy His will over our lives, churches, cities and nations with endurance. That's what Ezekiel did:

"So I prophesied as I was commanded. And as I prophesied, there was a noise and a shaking. And the bones came together, bone to its bone. When I looked, the sinews and the flesh grew upon them, and the skin covered them. But there was no breath in them" (Ezekiel 37:7-8).

MOVING TOWARD THE RESTORATION OF ALL THINGS

Look, when we're obedient to say what God tells us to say and to do what God tells us to do, we can expect things to change. Many feel the shaking in the nations right now and are believing the worst instead of the best. They are believing that everything is falling apart when really God is bringing it back together. We're moving rapidly toward the restoration of all things that God promised long ago through His holy prophets (see Acts 3:21).

Yes, Babylon will suddenly fall and be destroyed (see Jeremiah 51:8). Yes, an angel coming down from heaven, having great authority, will cry mightily with a loud voice, "Babylon the great is fallen, is fallen, and has become a dwelling place of demons, a prison for every foul spirit, and a cage for every unclean and hated bird!"

(see Revelation 18:1-2). Yes, everything that can be shaken will be shaken (see Hebrews 12:27).

That's why it's so important for the church to rise up and be the church in this hour. And we believe that is why God is raising up revival hubs. We need to wake ourselves up and wake up the lost to the reality of a God who saves, heals, delivers and restores. Encompassed with such a great cloud of witnesses, we need to lay aside every weight and the sin that so easily entangles us, and run with endurance the race that is set before us (see Hebrews 12:1). If we don't, the blood of many lost souls will be on our hands (see Ezekiel 3:18). We must prophesy as we are commanded and not be daunted by the shaking but press in harder. Revival hubs foster this type of culture. Ezekiel's vision ends this way:

"Then He said to me, 'Prophesy to the wind; prophesy, son of man, and say to the wind: Thus says the Lord God: Come from the four winds, O breath, and breathe upon these slain so that they live.' So I prophesied as He commanded me, and the breath came into them, and they lived and stood up upon their feet, an exceeding great army" (Ezekiel 37:9-10).

Again, we must prophesy what He commands. We must prophesy even if it looks like the mountain is too big to remove and be cast into the sea. We must do the work of an evangelist like it depends on us and pray like it depends on God. Revival hubs will breathe new life into the body of Christ and inspire us to stand up on our feet, an exceeding great army, and wage war against the principalities and powers that are trying to keep souls in bondage and take over nations.

A New Wineskin Holds New Wine

When Ezekiel prophesied to the bones, the result was a new structure, new skin and eventually new life. We can't prophesy to the dry bones and be surprised when a new wineskin emerges. God is shifting the wineskin.

God is raising up voices of prophetic revelation to speak to the old wineskin—not with judgment or criticism but in love and with the breath of life. See, if you put new wine in old wineskins it will break. When we pray for awakening or an outpouring but do not change the wineskin, we are asking for a spiritual force the current structure simply cannot handle. The old wineskin has already been stretched to its absolute limit—it's not pliable and cannot be used to hold new wine.

Jesus spoke of this: "No one sews a piece of new cloth on an old garment, or else the new piece that covered it tears away from the old, and the tear is made worse. And no one pours new wine into old wineskins, or else the new wine bursts the wineskins, and the wine is spilled, and the wineskins will be marred. But new wine must be poured into new wineskins" (Mark 9:21-22).

It is impossible for new wine to be effectively poured into an old wineskin. In this context the Holy Spirit is the wine. The Holy Spirit comes as rain (see Joel 2:23-29); as rivers (see John 7:37-39); as wind (see John 3:8); as oil (see 2 Corinthians 1:21-22); as fire (see Acts 2:3); as a dove (see Matt. 3:16). But He also comes as wine (see Ephesians 5:8).

What is this new wineskin as it relates to revival and awakening? A new paradigm of ministry that focuses on equipping rather than feeding, on sending rather than gathering, and on teams rather than a one-man- or one-woman-only model. We talked about some of those differences in chapter three and we'll explore the synergies of team ministry in chapter ten.

Again, it is impossible for the new wine to be effectively poured into old wineskins. The old wineskins simply cannot contain it. The new wine—the new ministry paradigm—breaks the mold of traditional ministry and, indeed, many traditional ministries reject this new wine altogether. The new wine is pouring over the foundations of the body of Christ and bringing a major shift. This is a large part of the reason the apostolic and prophetic gifts are vital to the emerging move—they are speaking to the foundations and shifting them.

Lee Grady, former editor of Charisma and director of The Mordecai Project, says he's willing to guess 90 percent of what we are doing in church today needs a total makeover. As he sees it, we are facing the most daunting renovation project in the history of the church. But, he says, the task is not impossible. He offers three painful steps to transitioning from the old wineskins to the new wineskins:

1. **We must break free from the fear of change.** "God is always on the move. He might lead us to camp in one spot for a while, but we can never get too comfortable in one place," says Grady. "His trumpet will eventually blow and the cloud of His presence will shift. Don't park when God is calling you forward. Stay open to His fresh directives, and expect Him to stretch your faith. He is adventurous!"

2. **We must be willing to defy tradition.** "People who are married to the past cannot embrace the future. Sacred cows do not belong in the pulpit; they must be sacrificed on the altar. 'The way we've always done it' will not work in God's new season," says Grady. "The crowd chooses the comfortable

pews of nostalgia, but God is with the courageous few who are willing to blaze a new path into unreached territory."

3. **We must ask the Spirit to reveal His new strategies.** "We cannot rely on church growth gurus, popular books or rock-star preachers to lead us into genuine change," says Grady. "Copying spiritual trends is just a form of carnality— and it is a sad substitute for real innovation. If the work of transforming the church is not totally led by the Holy Ghost, then our changes will be shallow and our impact will be pitiful. The last thing we need is a superficial upgrade."

This is Grady's conclusion and we agree: "I believe the Lord wants to unleash a gushing river of new wine into the church today, but He is directing us to prepare our wineskins. What is old must be renewed by the Spirit, what is outdated must be remodeled, and what is ineffective must be replaced. God wants to do a new thing. Don't resist it."

If you are reading this book, it's likely you are rushing into it, looking for definitions and strategies to confirm what the Holy Spirit has been showing you. In the next chapter, we'll share with you the most important strategy.

5

INTERCESSION: THE FOUNDATION
OF EVERY REVIVAL HUB

P rayer and intercession are the baseline—the foundation—of every revival hub. The very first outpouring of the Holy Ghost happened in an upper room where united believers were in constant prayer (see Acts 2:1-4)—and every other outpouring since has been preceded by strong intercession. A revival hub that is not built on the bedrock of intercession is no revival hub at all.

Samuel Chadwick, a 19th Century Wesleyan Methodist minister, said, "The one concern of the devil is to keep Christians from praying. He fears nothing from prayerless studies, prayerless work, and prayerless religion. He laughs at our toil, mocks at our wisdom, but trembles when we pray." And Matthew Henry, a 17th century minister and author, once said: "When God intends great mercy for His people, the first thing He does is to set them a-praying."

Jonathan Edwards, a revivalist preacher from the First Great Awakening, put it this way: "It is God's will through His wonderful grace, that the prayers of His saints should be one of the great principal means of carrying on the designs of Christ's Kingdom in the world.

When God has something very great to accomplish for His church, it is His will that there should precede it the extraordinary prayers of His people; as is manifest by Ezekiel 36:37 and it is revealed that, when God is about to accomplish great things for His church, He will begin by remarkably pouring out the spirit of grace and supplication (see Zechariah 12:10)."

These quotes probably make your spirit leap because you bear witness to the truth contained in such profound words. We've discovered many revivalists and intercessors are frustrated with the traditional church model that focuses more on programs than prayer. Indeed, intercession is a missing element in many churches today, but revival hubs, apostolic centers, houses of prayer, Kingdom centers and glory hubs put a high value on prayer. Revival hubs are filled with and fueled by praying people and prophetic intercession that unlocks apostolic strategies for the region, covers evangelists as they seek and save that which is lost, engages in high-level warfare, and otherwise handles Kingdom business.

PRAYER: THE FOUNDATION OF CHRIST'S MINISTRY

We get a picture of the foundation of Jesus' ministry as we examine His habits. Prayer is so important that Jesus put a premium on it. He ministered under great power and authority to the masses but then retreated to the presence of His Father. Communion with God was the absolute bedrock of all His exploits. Here's just one example:

"In the evening, when the sun had set, they brought to Him all who were sick and those who were possessed with demons. The whole city was gathered at the door, and He healed many who were sick with various diseases and cast out many demons. And He did not let the demons speak, because they knew Him" (Mark 1:32-35).

We know that Jesus prayed with others—He took Peter, John and James with Him to pray on a mountain (see Luke 9:28). We also know He prayed alone (see Luke 15:6). And it seems He liked to pray on and near mountains because Luke 6:12 gives record of Him praying at a mountainside. At least one time, He spent the whole night praying (see Luke 6:12). We know that Jesus often withdrew to lonely places to pray (Luke 5:16). In fact, Jesus is still making intercession for us (see Hebrews 7:25). Luke 11:1 recalls a time when Jesus "was praying in a certain place." When He was finished, His disciples asked Him to teach them how to pray. Jesus liked to pray in nature (see Psalm 19:1).

One of a revival hub's most critical missions is to establish a strong prayer center. Although each and every hub will function in it's own unique way, prayer must be the heartbeat. Of course, there are many different expressions of prayer ministry in the earth so prayer at one revival hub may look different than prayer at another revival hub. As long as it's all lifted up in the name of Jesus according to His will, it's all good.

Prayer should be a unifying force but the enemy often uses intercession as a weapon of division. Don't fall into the enemy's trap of letting prayer methodologies divide your tribe from another tribe. There are many different flows of corporate prayer and each one can be effective in touching the heart of God and bringing His will to earth as it is in heaven. Always remember, God is not as concerned with how we pray as if we pray. Prayer at its essence is communication with the Father and a full embrace of all that He is.

We see prayer teams, prayer rooms, houses of prayer, prayer centers, night watch prayer meetings and many other expression of corporate prayer arising in the earth in connection with revival hubs. Again, just as prayer was the foundation of Jesus' ministry on earth—and He still lives to make intercession for us—prayer must be the foundation of an effective revival hub.

Charles Haddon Spurgeon, a 19th Century British Particular Baptist preacher, once preached these words: "Oh, men and brethren, what would this heart feel if I could but believe that there were some among you who would go home and pray for a revival of religion— men whose faith is large enough, and their love fiery enough to lead them from this moment to exercise unceasing intercessions that God would appear among us and do wondrous things here, as in the times of former generations." Amen!

The Mandate for Day and Night Prayer

Day and night. Night and day. These are themes that run through the Bible—from Genesis to Revelation—and they are awakening the praying church to new realms of intercession. There is both biblical precedent and modern-day history for night and day prayer and we can see the fruit of it in Scripture. God's Word does not return to Him void, but it shall accomplish what He pleases and it shall prosper in the thing for which He sent it (see Isaiah 55:11). When we pray out His Word day and night, it will make an impact on the earth. It has to.

Day and night. We know that David, a prophetic worshipper, cried out to God day and night (see Psalm 88:1). That left a mark on his son and heir, Solomon. When Solomon finished rebuilding the temple—and when he finished his prayer of dedication—he blessed the assembly. In that blessing, he declared, "May these words of mine, with which I have made supplication before the Lord, be near the Lord our God day and night" (1 Kings 8:59). We know that Nehemiah prayed before the Lord, day and night, while he was rebuilding the wall (see Nehemiah 1:6). No matter what you are called to, day and night prayer is part of that calling and mature revival hubs will foster a culture of day and night prayer.

Day and night. Jesus made us a promise around prayer in the Parable of the Unjust Judge: "Shall God not avenge His own elect who cry out day and night to Him, though He bears long with them? I tell you that He will avenge them speedily ..." (Luke 18:7-8). No matter what the enemy has stolen from you—no matter what injustice God has called you to confront—day and night prayer is the means to invite God's righteous rule into the situation.

Night and day. Anna, an elderly prophetess, was one of the first to recognize the Messiah in the flesh. The Bible says she "did not depart from the temple, but served God with fastings and prayers night and day" (see Luke 2:37). We know that Paul prayed day and night for the Thessalonians (see 1 Thess. 3:9-11) and for his spiritual son Timothy (see 2 Tim. 1:3). Intercession for God's will upon the earth is a night and day work because our enemy never sleeps.

There is a long history of day and night prayer works in the earth. About 1,000 years before Christ came to the earth, David commanded that the Ark of the Covenant be carried into Jerusalem on the shoulders of the Levites and placed in a tent. He hired 288 prophetic singers and 4,000 musicians to minister before the Lord night and day (see 1 Chronicles 15:1–17:27).

In modern times, David Yonggi Cho, pastor of the Yoido Full Gospel Church in Seoul, South Korea, established Prayer Mountain with night and day prayer in 1973. In 1999, the International House of Prayer in Kansas City, Mo., started a worship-based prayer meeting that has continued for 24 hours a day, seven days a week since 1999.

Today, there are 24/7 houses of prayer and prayer mountains on every continent. Some of them are morphing into revival hubs. Some of them have the spirit of revival hubs. Some of them have always been revival hubs but didn't have the language to articulate the model.

INTERCESSION: THE WOMB OF REVIVAL

Revival hubs not only activate spiritual hunger and awakening in the life of an individual but also awaken the mandate of intercession. What is intercession? Simply stated, it is standing in the gap in prayer for another person, place, region, family or ministry. Intercession is the activity of prayer in which you give yourself over to spiritual warfare on behalf of another. Intercession is an aggressive wall of prayer pushing back the evil strategies of hell and unlocking the glorious exploits of heaven. It is in intercession that revival hubs congregants do battle for the assigned territory and people.

The Lord spoke Ryan and said, "I have plans for the land! Tell my people to find out my plan for the land and then stand and declare what I have already said." This is Scriptural. It lines up with Isaiah 55:11: "So shall My word be that goes forth from My mouth; it shall not return to Me void, but it shall accomplish that which I please, and it shall prosper in the thing for which I sent it." The picture of Isaiah 55:11 is a faith boomerang! You discover the word, speak it out and then it comes back with power and intensity manifesting the breakthrough. This is one of the keys missions of revival hubs.

God is establishing revival hubs in the earth to pray out His plans! He is calling forth a mighty army of prayer warriors to take on a prophetic spirit and see into the heavenly realms and pull the promises down. We call this process "Prophetic Discovery." You do what Habakkuk did and you climb the tower of prayer to see into the spirit (see Habakkuk 2:1). You discover the word of the Lord that is hovering over the land and give voice to it. Prophetic intercession teams boldly stand upon God's promises for the people, the city, the region—the nation. The promise provides direction. When prophetic discovery begins to happen in a place there is fuel added to the fire of revival.

We sense the Lord is calling forth the intercessors and the worshippers to stand before Him in faith decreeing Kingdom plans and purposes for the nations. Heaven shall touch earth but it rides the winds of prayer, worship and decree. There are spiritual plans and maps for every nation on earth in the corridors of heaven but it takes a people who will pray out the plans. We are believing for an activation of strategic prayer for people, regions and nations. We will stand and pray until God's glory invades the nations and awakening bursts forth.

Intercession is the womb of revival! People must become pregnant with purpose and pray the purpose out. There must be an activation of expectation and faith. Our joy is to enter realms of uncommon Holy Ghost intercession. When an atmosphere of prayer is established strange things can and will happen. Consider the Spirit-inspired words of Paul:

"Likewise, the Spirit helps us in our weaknesses, for we do not know what to pray for as we ought, but the Spirit Himself intercedes for us with groanings too deep for words. He who searches the hearts knows what the mind of the Spirit is, because He intercedes for the saints according to the will of God" (Romans 8:26-27).

There is a level of spirit prayer that can burst forth from someone's belly. When the Holy Spirit manifests with this level of intercession He is releasing a supernatural rescue mission! Deep intercessional groanings begin to break forth. The Holy Spirit takes over the prayer time in an unusual fashion. We are not talking about your normal prayer in other tongues for personal edification (see Jude 20). We are talking about something that comes in a moment of time and rises up from the very depths of your being. It is not something that you plan or control. It is a supernatural realm of the Spirit that manifests when God has need of you in a heightened level of prayer.

Some people ask, "Why bother praying?" They suggest that prayer rallies and solemn assemblies are a waste of time. We beg to differ. The only way we'll see a true transforming revival in this land is to pave the way for the King of glory to enter through our humble repentance, pursuit of the Lord in holiness, and desperate prayer.

INTERCESSION TURNS THE ATTACKS

Frank Sumrall, the son of the great general of deliverance Dr. Lester Sumrall, shared a powerful story about intercession with me (Ryan). Dr. Sumrall was on a preaching tour in the remote regions of Asia when he became deathly ill. He was on a long journey riding in a mule train (a long caravan of mules carrying people and supplies) when death began to grip him.

Dr. Sumrall felt the very life draining out of his body. He fell behind the rest of the caravan and eventually was isolated and was sure he was about to die. After praying and doing everything else he knew how to do, he fell to the ground. His body was slowly slipping into eternity. As he lay there expecting to die, the power of God came upon him. Dr. Sumrall rose completely healed and delivered supernaturally by the power of God.

When Dr. Sumrall returned to the United States, he shared his miraculous with some precious servants of God over dinner. The lady of the house was a powerful intercessor. After hearing his story, she retrieved her prayer journal. She asked him for the date and time the attack happened, then she showed him the contents of her prayer journal from that day. She had recorded how God revealed to her she was standing in the gap, fighting for his life. The Spirit of the Lord had burst forth from her belly in supernatural intercession. Here she was across the globe but on assignment from the Holy Spirit to rescue the life of one of His choice servants.

Intercession comes forth to turn the attacks! After James was killed, the early followers of Jesus were on high alert for persecution. When Peter was imprisoned, it seemed like he would suffer the same fate but intercession turned it around:

"About that time King Herod extended his hands to harm certain ones from the church. He killed James the brother of John with the sword. Seeing that it pleased the Jews, he proceeded further to arrest Peter also. This happened during the Days of Unleavened Bread. When he had seized him, he put him in prison and handed him over to four squads of soldiers to guard him, intending to bring him before the people after the Passover.

So Peter was kept in prison. But the church prayed to God without ceasing for him. The very night when Herod would have brought him out, Peter was sleeping between two soldiers, bound with two chains. And the guards before the door were securing the prison. And suddenly an angel of the Lord approached him, and a light shone in the prison. He struck Peter on the side and woke him up, saying, 'Rise up, quickly.' And the chains fell off his hands" (Acts 12:1-7).

The devil had plans to destroy the early church before it had been fully established and he wants to kill any revival before its flame is fully formed. In the Book of Acts, the devil attacked those called to father and pioneer and the devil is doing the same today. His strategies never change. The devil hates Kingdom plans, Kingdom purposes and Kingdom leaders. A man or woman who is carrying a vision, a revelation and the faith to bring it to pass is a threat to the enemy. If the devil can take you down then he can take your vision down.

In this account in the Book of Acts, Satan had already killed James and now he was coming after Peter. What was the response of the church? They entered into a heightened level of contending. They decided that they would not move off the promise of God. They would stand and declare God's will. They refused to allow Satan to be successful!

Know this: A spiritual war is raging over cities, regions and nations but each battle holds the potential of a massive treasure. Tremendous outpourings have been prophesied and declared in heaven but it is going to take apostolic and prophetic people willing to contend with principalities and powers to obtain the victory. There are Kingdom leaders who are carrying revival DNA for a region going through the fight of their life even now. Without a company of intercessors standing with them hell's forces may be successful in holding back the outpouring. We cannot and must not allow hell to take out choice men and women or defeat a vision before it is fully birthed.

BRINGING BACK THE OLD-SCHOOL INTERCESSORS

It's time to honor what some would call the old-school intercessors as we enter this new paradigm of ministry. Many churches have shut down intercession or relegated it a back room because it can get loud and messy. But old-school intercessors are vital to birthing and building revival hubs.

You know the story of revivalist Charles Finney. He was an attorney-turned-preacher in the early 1800s, declaring he received "a retainer from the Lord Jesus Christ to plead His cause." During his preaching days in New York, several revivals broke out and spread like wildfire. Finney was one of the first to allow women to pray in public. He was passionate about evangelism, had a mind for social reform and goes down in history as a catalyst for the Second Great Awakening.

You know Finney, but do you know Finney's intercessors? Fr. Daniel Nash and Abel Clary were old-school intercessors—intercessors who rose up long before the Pentecostal church was born—whom many credit with laying the foundation of the Finney-inspired revivals.

Although Finney's name is recorded in Christian history, fewer know anything about the dedication of Nash and Clary. Thankfully, we can still learn plenty from these mighty men of God if we dig deep enough into their prayer lives. We can learn what it means to be a true intercessor—and we can learn to value the gift of intercession and the people who walk in an anointing to pray without ceasing and bring heaven to earth.

Christ for All Nations evangelist Daniel Kolenda penned an article about Nash, explaining how Nash would precede Finney's arrival in a city for revival meetings. He was known to stay in his room for days at a time, interceding. Weeping and groaning could be heard coming from his room. Kolenda reports that Nash would not quit until he felt that the spiritual atmosphere had been prepared for Finney's arrival.

"The greatest moves of God in American history occurred during this season of time," Kolenda writes. "Entire regions were changed as a result of Finney's ministry. Historians point to those meetings as having such a profound impact upon people and societies that the effects could still be seen a century or more later! The powerful preaching of Charles Finney that saw hundreds of thousands of people saved would have never had the impact it did had it not been for the spiritual partnership with the intercessory ministry of Daniel Nash. It is interesting to note that only four months after Daniel Nash's death, Charles Finney left the itinerate revival ministry to pastor a church. The powerful revivals that characterized his ministry and changed a nation began to wane."

Abel Clary was just as able with intercession. Clary traveled with Finney everywhere Finney went. Finney himself wrote of Clary, "Mr. Clary continued as long as I did, and he did not leave until after I had left. He never appeared in public, but he gave himself wholly to prayer."

"[Clary] had been licensed to preach; but his spirit of prayer was such, he was so burdened with the souls of men, that he was not able to preach much, his whole time and strength being given to prayer," Finney wrote. "The burden of his soul would frequently be so great that he was unable to stand, and he would writhe in agony. I was well acquainted with him, and knew something of the wonderful spirit of prayer that rested upon him. He was a very silent man, as almost all are who have that powerful spirit of prayer."

As history tells it, Finney found Clary's prayer journal after Clary went on to glory. Recorded within its pages were the chronicles of the prayer burdens the Lord put on his heart. It's no accident or coincidence that those prayer burdens aligned, one by one, with the order of the blessings poured out on Finney's ministry and the people who came to his meetings.

It's rare that I meet these types of intercessors today—ones who lay down their lives for another. I know they exist, but based on the state of the church, the nation and the world, we discern a dearth of old-school intercessors like Nash and Clary in the modern age. For if there were more like Nash and Clary, we convinced there would be more revivals, more salvations—even another Great Awakening. We're calling them forth right now, in Jesus name. Intercessors, we value and honor the gift of intercession that you carry. You are much needed in the revival hub paradigm.

6

Prophetic Worship: Releasing the Sound of Heaven

We are convinced that prophetic worship and new sounds are a vital part of the emerging move of God. It's time to transition from the house of Saul to the house of David, who gave birth to a new level of prophetic worship in his generation.

Think about it for a minute. The songs and sounds of the Lord were part of His cutting-edge battle plans in Joshua's day (see Joshua 6) and Jehoshaphat's day (see 2 Chronicles 20). And we know whenever an evil spirit came upon Saul, David would play his prophetic worship and it departed from him (see 1 Samuel 16:23).

Spontaneous prophetic praise and worship also broke out after great victories. Miriam sang a new song after the Israelites escaped the oppression of Egypt (see Exodus 15:21). After David killed Goliath—something no other warrior in Israel was even willing to try—the nation's women danced and sang, "Saul has slain his thousands, and David his ten thousands" (1 Samuel 18:7). And Deborah broke out into prophetic song after the Israelites defeated

Sisera (see Judges 5).

David understood the power of prophetic worship perhaps better than anyone. That's why he raised up a prayer and worship model, which we now call the Tabernacle of David. David filled his kingdom with God's glory 24/7. He had 4,000 gatekeepers and 4,000 singers and musicians that "offer praises to the Lord with the instruments" (see 1 Chronicles 23:5).

Today, we long to see the restoration of the tabernacle of David. Amos prophesied, "On that day I will raise up the tabernacle of David, which has fallen down, and repair its damages; I will raise up its ruins, and rebuild it as in the days of old" (Amos 9:11, NKJV). The Holy Spirit reminds us of this promise in the Book of Acts: "After this I will return, and I will rebuild the tabernacle of David, which has fallen; I will rebuild its ruins, and I will set it up; that the rest of men may seek the Lord, and all the Gentiles who are called by My name" (Acts 15:16-17).

With these prophetic promises in mind, we believe there is another era of Davidic worship coming forth in this generation. It is in the release of the sounds, songs and passionate worship that revival comes breaking forth! We see a generation of musical prophets arising in the land, armed with instruments of battle and glory filling the house with the sounds of heaven.

THE HEART OF PROPHETIC WORSHIP

Before we go any further, let's make sure we're on the same page. What is prophetic worship? Simply stated, it is singing, playing and ministering under the inspiration of the Holy Spirit. It is releasing spontaneous or new sounds and songs. Prophetic worship in its purest form reflects God's glory in us so that others can see and know His love. Prophetic worship connects our hearts with the heart of God.

Jesus said, "Yet the hour is coming, and is now here, when the true worshippers will worship the Father in spirit and truth. For the Father seeks such to worship Him. God is Spirit, and those who worship Him must worship Him in spirit and truth" (John 4:22-24).

Prophetic worship may be the height of worshipping in Spirit and truth because the Spirit of Truth—the Holy Spirit who leads and guides us into all truth—is giving testimony of Jesus. And the spirit of prophecy is the testimony of Jesus (see Revelation 19:10). The Holy Spirit, a prophetic spirit, always exalts Jesus. In the same way, prophetic worship exalts Jesus.

True prophetic worship can do one or any of these 13 things:

1. Release and reveal the heart of the Father,
2. Capture a moment of adoration and lift it higher,
3. Release impartations from God,
4. Break open the heavens over a people and territory,
5. Release healing power,
6. Push back and break the power of the enemy,
7. Release deliverance and breakthrough,
8. Prepare hearts to receive the Word of God,
9. Sing forth the redemptive plans of God and love of the Father,
10. Release the sounds of the Lord,
11. Bring forth new sounds,
12. Loose revival fire and glory,
13. Prepare hearts for life-changing counters with God.

This is not an exhaustive list. God can and likely does many other things in prophetic worship atmospheres that we cannot even discern, articulate or understand.

"Prophetic worship is a distinct characteristic of Brazilian worship. We not only sing worship songs to God, but we also sing our prayers—especially prayers for the healing of our nation," says Ana Paula Valadao, an award-winning worship artist and founder of the music ministry Diante do Trono (Before the Throne).1 "We have many native songs in which we cry out for the healing and restoration of our families, our government, our economy—and these songs often have preceded a move of God, as they've literally broken open the heavenly realm."

In the dimension of prophetic worship, we're singing to the Lord, singing forth His plans and purposes, decreeing and declaring His will—and more. And at times it feels like He's also singing over us: "The Lord your God is in your midst, a Mighty One, who will save. He will rejoice over you with gladness, He will renew you with His love, He will rejoice over you with singing" (Zephaniah 3:17).

Prophetic Worship: An Earmark of Revival Hubs

We've already established that revival hubs are an expression of a church that is positioned to pray in the next great move of God, then reach out of its four walls with evangelism strategies and an equipping dimension complete with impartation, activation and sending. Prophetic worship plays a vital role in establishing this culture. At least one third of our corporate worship experience should be in a prophetic flow.

Where do we get that? It's not a man-made idea. Ephesians 5:19 says, "Speak to one another in psalms, hymns, and spiritual songs, singing and making melody in your heart to the Lord." According to this verse, at least one third of our corporate worship time should be spontaneous! Yet how many church gatherings do we attend at which every moment of the worship is meticulously planned like a majestic performance?

Young revival hubs can struggle to establish a paradigm where spontaneous worship, new song and prophetic music flow freely. Nurturing a culture of prophetic worship is challenging, in part, because there seems to be a war within the church over musicians. Some churches keep tight control over worship ministry and others are threatened by houses of prayer, revival hubs and other alternative expressions of the church and discourage their musicians from getting involved in these settings.

Don't be discouraged if this describes your situation. Lift up your praise and worship and believe God that He's sending you the right team with the right sound at the right time. You'll have to pray in— you'll have to contend—for your prophetic minstrels and singers. Then you'll have to cover them in prayer because they are on the front lines of the battle for a great awakening.

Again, prophetic worship plays a vital role in revival hubs. Prophetic worship is seeking the heart of God for a moment, a service and releasing His agenda through music—pouring our hearts out before Him with spontaneous worship songs, and receiving His heart for us. Music sets the stage for prophecy. We see examples of this in Bible:

"After that you will come to the hill of God, where the garrison of the Philistines is. And when you come there to the city, you will meet a group of prophets coming down from the high place with a harp, a tambourine, a flute, and a lyre before them. And they will prophesy" (1 Samuel 10:5).

"Elisha said, 'As the Lord of Hosts lives, before whom I stand, surely, were it not for my regard for Jehoshaphat the king of Judah, I would not look at you nor see you. Now bring me a musician.' And when the musician played, the hand of the Lord came upon him. He said, "Thus says the Lord 'Make this valley full of pools'" (2 Kings 14:16).

"Then David and the officers of the army also set apart for the service some of the sons of Asaph, and of Heman, and of Jeduthun, those who prophesied with lyres, harps, and cymbals. The number of those who did the work according to their service was: From the sons of Asaph: Zakkur, Joseph, Nethaniah, and Asarelah, the sons of Asaph under the guidance of Asaph, who prophesied according to the decree of the king. For Jeduthun, the sons of Jeduthun: Gedaliah, Zeri, Jeshaiah, Hashabiah, and Mattithiah, six, under the guidance of their father Jeduthun, who prophesied with the lyre in giving thanks and praise to the Lord" (1 Chronicles 15:1-5).

Some minstrels and psalmists carry a prophetic gift, which is vital in the hour that we are living in. We need a musical expression of God's heart. We need meetings and gatherings where prophetic realms are unlocked and we here Daddy's heart. It takes prophetic worship to reach this level in the spirit.

If you are a young revival hub, you may have to do what you can with what you have, but as you build your team remember this: There is a blessing upon preparation and excellence. When David was selecting men to lead worship and Israel the Bible tells us that he chose skilled musicians (see 1 Chronicles 25:7). When God gives us a gift or talent we should do all that we can to excel and operate in an excellent spirit. Yet preparation and excellence should not override the power of God.

The Power Pillars: Worship, Prayer and Glory

We are admonished to sing spiritual songs. This is part of prophetic worship. Worship, prayer and glory are the power pillars! Combining these three releases a supernatural atmosphere that builds faith for the impossible. You might say we step into a dimension of heaven on earth. Consider this scene from heaven:

"The four living creatures had six wings each, and they were covered with eyes all around. All day and night, without ceasing, they were saying: 'Holy, holy, holy, Lord God Almighty,' who was, and is, and is to come. When the living creatures give glory and honor and thanks to Him who sits on the throne, who lives forever and ever, the twenty-four elders fall down before Him who sits on the throne, and worship Him, who lives forever and ever. Then they cast their crowns before the throne, saying,

'You are worthy, O Lord, to receive glory and honor and power; for You have created all things, and by Your will they exist and were created" (Revelation 4:8-11).

In these verses we get a powerful picture of the ongoing night and day reverence of God in heaven. This is the pattern of the glory: continual praises going up, prayers being offered, and glory filling the atmosphere. This is Scriptural. In the Lord's Prayer, Jesus taught us to pray: "Your kingdom come; Your will be done on earth, as it is in heaven" (Matthew 6:10).

This is the declaration we should manifest heaven on earth! The Bible gives us a clear pattern for prayer. As ambassadors of Christ, we are charged with bringing a throne room atmosphere to earth. When we lift up prayers and magnify His name, the glory of God will come down. The weighty presence of God begins to move and we enter a supernatural dimension. One of the primary Hebrew words for glory is *kabob* and one of its meanings is "weight." When we press into prophetic praise and worship and prayer, a weighty glory overwhelms the natural and causes the kingdom to burst forth with power and authority. In the glory, bondages melt like wax. In the glory, fear is instantly removed. In the glory, man's ways bow.

Again, our joy is to bring a throne room atmosphere to earth. The Lord said this to Isaiah: "Heaven is My throne, and the earth is My footstool. Where then is the house that you could build for Me? And where is the place of My rest?" (Isaiah 66:1). God's throne is the seat of governmental authority, power and majesty. The Father wants to establish places on earth that mirror the atmosphere of heaven. Places where unashamed worship arises with passion and sincerity. The throne room is filled with sounds of adoration.

Something happens in a territory when the sounds of heaven are released. The rise of new songs pushes back the darkness and releases the powerful victory of heaven. God's throne room authority begins to flow. People are supernaturally healed and set free in glory-filled worship encounters. Worship leader Catherine Mullins said it this way: "God responds to the praises of His people. We praise and He fights for us." We have been in revival meetings where prophetic worship and praise went to such a high level you could almost hear the sounds of chains breaking off people in the spirit realm.

In her book *Releasing Heaven's Song: Singing Over Your Nation for Breakthrough and Revival*, Australian Christian artist Roma Waterman says the reason that the new song is so powerful is because it can be many things at the same time. It is fresh, new, she says, yet is also a repaired and restored sound.

"It can be something that is spontaneous, yet it also can be a structured song. Both have been inspired from the Holy Spirit. It is a sound that is fresh and exciting but at the same time can also sound familiar or sound like 'home.' It can be a song written and released for the right moment in time, yet be sung 100 years later, much like the hymns of Charles or John Wesley are still be relevant and fresh," Waterman says.

"Don't underestimate the power of the new song and what is can do in the hearts of the people and yourself. Don't dismiss something because it is old or has been 'done before,' yet at the same time, don't dismiss that which is new and unfamiliar. The new song is everywhere and ready for all who have ears to hear and mouths to sing."

For too long we have been stuck in a rut concerning worship. We do not see the level of glory that God wants to release. As we saw with Elijah, the minstrel creates an atmosphere that opens up a prophetic realm (see 2 Kings 14:16). There are revival hubs rising in territories that need people with the minstrel anointing to help open up the prophetic realm over the territory.

Raw prophetic worship releases glory, power and demonstration of the Spirit. God values spontaneity and obedience. It takes faith and passion to step out and sing a new song. It takes trusting God and radically pursuing His heart to move in a moment of prophetic worship. All the planning and preparation should be to usher in the Father's presence.

Our gatherings must value moments of spontaneous eruption and expression. Worship in this emerging move of God will look much more like a prayer room with radical pursuit, songs and sounds from the secret place and total abandon. Gone are the days of looking and sounding good for a performance. The sound of this emerging move is one that is authentic, sincere and refreshingly prophetic.

There is a generation of Davids arising who will lead the worship at the revival hubs. They are men and women who have walked alone for a season, misunderstood and hidden for an appointed time. In their wilderness experience they have chosen to focus on the presence of a man named Jesus! They are dripping with His presence and they bring fresh oil every time they occupy a place of worship. They know how to tap the heavenly realms and they are not afraid to go after God full throttle in the midst of others. They announce healings in spontaneous songs. They release affirming words of the Father's love over people. They capture and move in moments of rich adoration of the Father. They are a new breed destined to bring forth a new sound!

In the next chapter, we'll take a look at revival tribes. Are you in one? If not, how can you find one?

1 Charisma magazine article: How Prophetic Worship Can Change a Nation (http://www.charismamag.com/spirit/evangelism-missions/18091-how-prophetic-worship-can-shape-a-nation)

7

ESTABLISHING REVIVAL TRIBES

"I am establishing revival tribes in the land."

The Holy Spirit spoke those words to me (Ryan).
"As prophetic intercession and worship goes forth, it will draw hungry believers who want to press in to what God is saying in this hour. Revival tribes— people of like-precious faith that are determined to see God move in this generation—will begin to emerge."

When you think of tribes, you may think of Native American tribes or even the animal kingdom. Maybe you've never heard that term "tribe" in a spiritual setting beyond the 12 tribes of Israel. Let's take a moment to explore this concept, then we'll show you some revival tribes in Scripture that will give you a new perspective on what God is doing among revival-minded people in this hour. You've probably already experienced this, but may not have a definition for what you are walking in.

Merriam-Webster defines the word tribe as "a group of people that includes many families and relatives who have the same language, customs and beliefs; a large family; a group of people who have the same job or interest." Now let's put that into the context of revival. We could say that a revival tribe is a group of people that includes many spiritual families or spiritual relatives who speak the same spiritual language—the language of prayer, fasting, prophetic worship, revival and awakening.

Revival tribes have the same customs. Customs are defined as "actions and ways of behaving that are usual and traditional among the people in a particular group or place; something that is done regularly by a person; a repeated practice." The customs of revival hubs include contending for awakening, reaching the lost, equipping the saints for the work of the ministry, and so on.

Revival tribes have the same beliefs. Beliefs are defined as "a feeling of being sure that someone or something exists or that something is true; a feeling that something is good, right or valuable; a feeling of trust in the worth or ability of someone." Revival tribes may not have the same denominational backgrounds. Revival tribes may not agree on every point of theology. But revival tribes are sure that Jesus, the Lord of the Harvest, is going to bring another Great Awakening to the land. They value efforts to facilitate the next great move of God and trust each other as they co-labor with Christ to that end.

Hearts Knit Together

A revival tribe is a spiritual family knit together by the Holy Ghost and established in the call of revival and awakening. Put another way, a revival tribe is not joined together by a title, by a theology or a name. It is a group that relates as a family.

This is a vital revolution in ministry paradigm because many people build churches or ministries based solely on agreement over what needs to happen in a region. Here's the problem with that: As the ministry evolves or takes on a new prophetic task, people fall out of agreement with the vision and suddenly abandon the group. A family is knit together by common DNA and covenant love. They continue on the journey even if there is a disagreement over minor matters of executing the vision.

Again, revival tribes are built on the foundation of a spiritual family. In revival tribes, you'll find spiritual fathers and mothers; spiritual sons and daughters; and spiritual brothers and sisters. Revival tribes are made up of people whose hearts are knit together for a common purpose. Paul made that first point clear in his letter to the Colossians. Paul wrote this epistle to Christians in Colossae in about AD 60. These Christians were part of the first real Great Awakening, or the result of the first coming of Christ.

As a spiritual father, Paul was essentially speaking to a revival tribe in Colassae when he said, "I would like you to know what a great struggle I am having for you, and for those at Laodicea, and for everyone who has not seen my face in the flesh, that their hearts may be comforted, being knit together in love, and receive all the riches and assurance of full understanding, and knowledge of the mystery of God, both of the Father and of Christ, in whom are hidden all the treasures of wisdom and knowledge" (Colossians 2:1-3).

Paul prayed that God would knit their hearts together in love. We also see how Paul relates to a key member of his own revival tribe, his spiritual son Timothy. We know that Paul encouraged Timothy time and time again in two very personal letters. He called him "my true son in the faith" (1 Timothy 1:2). Paul gathered spiritual sons around him, including Timothy and Titus, as he traveled. This was more than an apostolic company; this was his spiritual family. Paul and Timothy had an enduring bond that navigated seasons of great blessing and power but also seasons of adversity and challenge. But notice how the tribe was formed in the going:

"Then he came to Derbe and then to Lystra. A disciple was there, named Timothy, the son of a Jewess who believed, but his father was a Greek. He was well spoken of by the brothers who were at Lystra and Iconium. Paul wanted him to travel with him. So he took him and circumcised him because of the Jews who were in those places, for they all knew that his father was a Greek. As they went through the cities, they delivered to them the decrees to observe, that were set forth by the apostles and elders at Jerusalem. So the churches were strengthened in the faith, and increased in number daily" (Acts 16:1-5).

REVIVAL TRIBES WAR TOGETHER

We'll talk more about spiritual warfare in a later chapter, but it's important to note that revival tribes war together. Think about the tribes of Israel: Reuben, Simeon, Judah, Issachar, Zebulun, Benjamin, Dan, Naphtali, Gad, Asher, Ephraim and Manasseh. Each tribe had different earmarks but they had one common purpose: to move into God's Promised Land. Of course, that often meant war.

When the Lord told Moses to "Avenge the children of Israel on the Midiantes," (Numbers 31:1), he sent 1,000 from each of the 12 tribes to war. Our revival tribes may have different expressions—some may be more apostolic than prophetic and others may be more teaching- or prayer-oriented—but they all have one thing in common: to move into a Third Great Awakening.

After Joshua took the Israelites into the Promised Land and defeated the enemies, he divided up the land according to tribes. God is even now appointing revival leaders in various regions of the nation—and the nations of the earth—to lead revival tribes that have an anointing to work the works of God in their spheres of influence.

Your sphere of influence is your *metron*, the Greek word for "measure." Paul told the Corinthians: "But we will not boast beyond measure, but within the boundaries which God has appointed us, which reach even you. For we are not overextending ourselves as though we did not reach you, since we have come to you, preaching the gospel of Christ" (2 Corinthians 10:13-14). Find your tribe. Find your metron. Press into the warfare with the expectation of victory. Joshua 19:47 speaks of a time the tribe of Dan lost its territory and had to go to war against Leshem. When they united in battle, they recaptured the land.

The Israelites went to war together—and unfortunately sometimes against one another. The tribe of Judah and the tribe of Benjamin assembled 180,000 chosen men who were warriors to fight against the house of Israel and bring the kingdom back to Rehoboam, the son of Solomon, after he died (1 Kings 12:21). We must not allow strife to enter our revival tribes. We must not allow power struggles in our spiritual family—or among other revival tribes. We're all laboring for the same end goal: to enter God's promised awakening.

DAVID'S REVIVAL TRIBE

When God wanted to transition Israel from an old wineskin to a new wineskin—from Saul to David—there was a remnant who saw and agreed with God's plan. It's the same way today. God is introducing a new wineskin to the church paradigm. Revival hubs serve the purpose of a church in the sense that they gather believers, worship, pray, and teach, but they add another dimension that's been lacking in many churches—a dimension that revival-minded believers are hungry for and, we believe, a dimension that will undergird the next great move of God. That dimension is a desperation for God that He cannot resist.

David's revival tribe wasn't sophisticated but it was sold out to the vision. We see this in the cave of Adullam: "There gathered to him every one that was in distress, and every one in debt, and every one that was discontented. So he became captain over them. Now there were with him about four hundred men" (1 Samuel 22:2). These men were desperate!

David started his revival tribe with a desperate remnant. His revival tribe was made up of everyone that was in distress, in debt and discontented. Your revival tribe will form because of discontentment with church as usual and will continue to attract the distressed, in debt and discontent. The good news is revival hubs stir a hunger for more of God; they are places for hungry people to come and receive. Psalm 107:9 promises, "He satisfies the longing soul and fills the hungry soul with goodness." Those coming into your revival tribe will become content, but never satisfied—always pressing into more of God.

A revival tribe carries the DNA of revival and awakening. Revival-hungry believers corporately long for something more than church-as-usual. They share a common desperation in the spirit. Prayer and worship is marked with the sounds of longing. Revival tribes are change agents. They join together in faith, prayer and seeking to see radical transformation. They are not content to just have good meetings or build a "nice" ministry.

Revival tribes are charged with radical obedience. They are a people who move under the wind of God. When the Father says go, they go. They are unafraid of change and transition because their hearts are set on pleasing and obeying the Heavenly Father. They follow the Holy Spirit at all costs. They pray without ceasing (see 1 Thessalonians 5:17).

In the next chapter we'll explore another facet of revival hubs— revival tribes press into the supernatural.

8

PRESSING INTO THE SUPERNATURAL

The supernatural is flowing in dribs and drabs in the church today, but Jesus was crystal clear when He said signs would follow those who believe. It's supposed to be natural for us to cast out demons, speak with new tongues, lay hands on the sick and see them recover and witness various other signs (see Mark 16:17).

And if that's not evidence enough, Paul told the Corinthians twice to earnestly desire spiritual gifts (see 1 Corinthians 12:31; 1 Corinthians 14:1). Revival hub congregants will pray into, preach about, teach on and move in supernatural realms as the body matures in faith. Although some have gifts of healings and others have prophecy or some other gift—are called to move in a supernatural element.

"But the manifestation of the Spirit is given to everyone for the common good. To one is given by the Spirit the word of wisdom, to another the word of knowledge by the same Spirit, to another faith by the same Spirit, to another gifts of healings by the same Spirit, to another the working of miracles, to another prophecy, to another discerning of spirits, to another various kinds of tongues, and to another the interpretation of tongues. But that one and very same

Spirit works all these, dividing to each one individually as He will" (1 Corinthians 12:7-11).

You don't get to pick and choose which gift you want, but you can earnestly desire spiritual gifts and believe the Holy Spirit to give you the gift or gifts what He wants you to flow in. Revival hub leaders will help believers discover their spiritual gifts and release them to flow with the Holy Spirit, providing a safe place to exercise the gifts before getting sent out into the highways and byways with the supernatural power of God following.

IT'S TIME TO PRESS IN FOR MIRACLES

Katherine Kuhlman once spoke of miracle-provoking faith. We need more miracle-provoking faith in this hour. In fact, if we expect an apathetic lukewarm Western church to wake up—or if we expect to see a great harvest of hardened, lost souls come into the Kingdom— we must contend for the supernatural. When we preach a pure gospel, we can expect the Lord to work with us, confirming the word with accompanying signs (see Mark 16:20). Look at this example:

"Therefore those who were scattered went everywhere preaching the word. Philip went down to the city of Samaria and preached Christ to them. When the crowds heard Philip and saw the miracles which he did, they listened in unity to what he said. For unclean spirits, crying with a loud voice, came out of many who were possessed. And many who were paralyzed or lame were healed. So there was much joy in that city" (Acts 8:4-8).

Notice that the signs followed the preaching of the gospel. The Gospels and the Book of Acts are overflowing with miracles. If you read Mark, an action-oriented account of Jesus' ministry on earth, you see miracle after miracle after miracle—after miracle. Acts 10:38

tells us, "How God anointed Jesus of Nazareth with the Holy Spirit and with power, who went about doing good and healing all who were oppressed by the devil, for God was with Him."

God is with us in the same way God was with Jesus—and in the same way God was with Philip, Peter, John, Paul, Moses, Elijah, Elisha and many others who had miracle ministries. In this hour, we need to press into extraordinary miracles like Paul did: "And God did unusual and extraordinary miracles by the hands of Paul, So that handkerchiefs or towels or aprons which had touched his skin were carried away and put upon the sick, and their diseases left them and the evil spirits came out of them" (Acts 19:11, AMP).

Revival hubs create an atmosphere for the miraculous through strong intercession, prophetic worship and an attitude that contends for revival. Unlike traditional churches that are strictly formatted on a timeline, revival hub leaders do not allow time to constrain God. If the Holy Spirit leads the body into worship for eight hours, we worship. If a healing service breaks out, we flow with it. Revival hubs take the limits off God while staying rooted and grounded in the Word of God.

CATCHING THE MIRACLE-WORKING ANOINTING

As a believer, you have authority in Christ and you have an anointing from the Holy Ghost. John said, "You have an anointing from the Holy One" (1 John 2:20) and again "The anointing which you have received from Him remains in you" (1 John 2:27). The Greek word for anointing in these words is "chrisma" and it means, "anything smeared on, unguent, ointment, usually prepared by the Hebrews from oil and aromatic herbs."

Of course, we know that it's not literal oil but the anointing of the Holy Spirit. The anointing is God's ability in you to help you do something with ease. The anointing is the power of God. There are anointings for preaching, teaching, healing, deliverance, prophetic expressions, praise and worship, favor and so on. You are anointed!

"On the last and greatest day of the feast, Jesus stood and cried out, 'If anyone is thirsty, let him come to Me and drink. He who believes in Me, as the Scripture has said, out of his heart shall flow rivers of living water.' By this He spoke of the Spirit, whom those who believe in Him would receive. For the Holy Spirit was not yet given, because Jesus was not yet glorified" (John 7:37-39).

The anointing is the yoke destroying force of heaven (see Isaiah 10:27.) The anointing sets the captives free. Remember this: The anointing is not just taught but caught. In other words, studying the anointing can build faith for the anointing but you can catch something by sitting under the anointing that brings another dimension to the equation. Believers have an anointing! It was passed from Jesus to the 10, then the 70, then to all believers.

Developing Faith for the Anointing

So how do you develop faith for the anointing? There are Scriptural keys and practical insights we can share. First, faith must be targeted. Jesus said, "For truly I say to you, whoever says to this mountain, 'Be removed and be thrown into the sea,' and does not doubt in his heart, but believes that what he says will come to pass, he will have whatever he says" (Mark 11:23). Identify your mountain and target it with your faith. Use your faith to stir the gifts and the anointing that abides in you.

Next, faith must be built. Jude 20 explains, "But you, beloved, build yourselves up in your most holy faith. Pray in the Holy Spirit."

Pray in the Holy Spirit as much and as often as you can. This is a key to building your faith, stirring the anointing and unlocking revelation in your life that further builds your faith. Paul told the Corinthians, "I thank my God that I speak in tongues more than you all" (1 Corinthians 14:18).

Paul told the Romans, "So then faith comes by hearing, and hearing by the word of God" (Romans 10:17). Meditate on the Scriptures about the anointing. Dive into the miracles of Jesus and the accounts in the Book of Acts. Watch YouTube videos from the Voice of Healing evangelists like Jack Coe, Oral Roberts and A.A. Allen. Read biographies of men and women of God with great healing ministries like Kathryn Kuhlman and John G. Lake.

Faith must also be released. You release your faith by speaking and doing. Faith without works is dead (see James 2:17). Faith requires action. Faith is now (see Hebrews 11:11). What can you do right now that would demonstrate your faith? How can you put your faith to work? Here's one way: If you stay sensitive to the Holy Spirit and He tells you He wants to heal your coworker, step out in faith and ask your coworker if you can pray for them. When the Holy Spirit wants to work a miracle, He'll usually move through the obedient action of people. Let that person be you!

The Apostle Paul defines faith as "being sure of what we hope for and certain of what we do not see" (Hebrews 11:1). We like 18th century revivalist John Wesley's paraphrase of this verse: "[Faith] is the power to see into the world of spirits, into things invisible and eternal. It is the power to understand those things which are not perceived by worldly senses."

MOVING IN REVELATION

You need revelation to move in the supernatural. You need the spirit of revelation. You need to tap into knowledge that's revealed by light in your inner man as you set out to operate in spiritual gifts like the word of knowledge, gifts of healings, gift of prophecy, and working of miracles, discerning of spirits, interpretation of tongues, word of wisdom and gift of faith.

Paul told the church at Corinth: "For he who speaks in an unknown tongue does not speak to men, but to God. For no one understands him, although in the spirit, he speaks mysteries" (1 Cor. 14:2). The miracle-working apostle went on to say:

"But we speak the wisdom of God in a mystery, the hidden wisdom, which God ordained before the ages for our glory. None of the rulers of this age knew it. For had they known it, they would not have crucified the Lord of glory. But as it is written, 'Eye has not seen, nor ear heard, nor has it entered into the heart of man the things which God has prepared for those who love Him. 'But God has revealed them to us by His Spirit.

"For the Spirit searches all things, yes, the deep things of God. For what man knows the things of a man, except the spirit of man which is in him? Likewise, no one knows the things of God, except the Spirit of God. Now we have received not the spirit of the world, but the Spirit which is of God, so that we might know the things that are freely given to us by God. These things also we proclaim, not in the words which man's wisdom teaches, but which the Holy Spirit teaches, comparing spiritual things with spiritual" (1 Corinthians 2:7-13).

Pray this apostolic prayer over yourself daily, reformatting it into the first person:

"[For I always pray to] the God of our Lord Jesus Christ, the Father of glory, that He may grant you a spirit of wisdom and revelation [of insight into mysteries and secrets] in the [deep and intimate] knowledge of Him, by having the eyes of your heart flooded with light, so that you can know and understand the hope to which He has called you, and how rich is His glorious inheritance in the saints (His set-apart ones), And [so that you can know and understand] what is the immeasurable and unlimited and surpassing greatness of His power in and for us who believe, as demonstrated in the working of His mighty strength" (Ephesians 1:17-19 AMP).

SEEING THE INVISIBLE, DOING THE IMPOSSIBLE

If you can see the invisible, you can do the impossible. Although we walk by faith and not by sight, if we can see it in the spirit—if we have a vision for the miraculous in our paradigm—we can move into it. Just as we prophesy according to our faith, we do the impossible by faith. And if we believe it, we'll declare it—and as we declare God's will in a territory He will confirm His Word with signs following (see Mark 16:20). Let this passage of Scripture encourage your faith:

"We have the same spirit of faith. As it is written, 'I believed, and therefore I have spoken.' So we also believe and therefore speak, knowing that He who raised the Lord Jesus will also raise us through Jesus and will present us with you. All these things are for your sakes, so that the abundant grace through the thanksgiving of many might overflow to the glory of God. For this reason we do not lose heart: Even though our outward man is perishing, yet our inward man is being renewed day by day. Our light affliction, which lasts but for a moment, works for us a far more exceeding and eternal weight of glory, while we do not look at the things which are seen, but at the things which are not seen. For the things which are seen are temporal, but the things which are not seen are eternal" (2 Corinthians 4:13-18).

Can you see it? Are you gaining a vision to move in the miraculous? Read the Book of Acts. Read the Gospels. Read the exploits of Elijah and Elisha. You'll find miracle after miracle there. Read these accounts out loud because faith comes by hearing (see Romans 10:17). Watch old YouTube videos of Oral Roberts, A.A. Allen, Katherine Kuhlman and others that we've archived on AwakeningTV.com—and cry out to God for Him to use you in the same way for His glory. Between the two of us, we've seen terminal cancer healed. We've seen deaf ears open and blind eyes see. We've seen various diseases healed, ache and pains go, and on and on and on. In this hour, some are even seeing the dead raised. What's stopping you from raising the dead?

Raising the Dead in Jesus' Name!

Heart specialist Dr. Chauncey Crandall was attending to his patients when he was summoned to the emergency room. He knew his presence on the scene was not only a last resort, but also most likely a lost cause. Markin's heart rhythm had flat-lined with cardiac arrest from a massive heart attack. A full 40 minutes had come and gone since his heart beat last. His pupils were fixed and dilated—he'd been "down" too long.

By the time Crandall arrived at the emergency room, Markin's heart had already been shocked six times with the defibrillator. Just to make sure, his non-beating heart received a seventh shock, also to no avail. Rounds of medication and other efforts had all failed to revive the patient. Markin's lips, fingers and toes had literally turned black with death from a lack of oxygen. There was no doubt—he was dead.

After Markin died, nearly everyone left the room. Nobody wants to remain around the smells and specter of death. While a nurse prepared Markin's lifeless body for the morgue, Crandall remained in the room to write up his final report. Then, once he completed his paperwork, he headed toward the door to return to his patients.

Standing in the door's threshold, however, he was overcome with a strong feeling—a deep-seated sense that God wanted him to turn around and pray for Markin. At first, Crandall—a man of science— was somewhat reluctant, even embarrassed. He felt foolish. But the request from God came to Crandall again, even more compelling this time. So he felt called to heed the message. As Crandall put it, he felt like "God's intercom."

And even though the words Crandall said came through him, he had no sense of devising them—they poured from him of their own accord. "Father God," Crandall prayed, "I cry out for this man's soul. If he does not know You as his Lord and Savior, raise him from the dead now, in Jesus' name." Then another strange thing happened. Involuntarily, Crandall's right arm shot up in a gesture of prayer and praise.

At that moment, the ER doctor came back into the room, and Crandall ordered him to give Markin what seemed like one more useless shock from the defibrillator. At first reluctant, the doctor finally did as Crandall asked and applied the defibrillator.

Immediately, the machine registered a perfect heartbeat. Markin started breathing on his own. His black, cyanotic toes and fingers twitched. Soon, he began to mumble.

Jeff Markin had returned from the dead.

Jesus used Robby Dawkins, pastor of Vineyard Church in Aurora,

Illinois, to raise a man from the dead. He battled the spirit of death and won. His advice to those believing to move in miracles—and even raise the dead—is this: "Pray for the dead to be raised every time. Thinking you have to have a word to raise the dead, heal the sick, or even give a prophetic word is slavery mentality. Live like heirs and more than conquerors, not slaves. Don't trust your feelings, they can lie to you. Trust what Jesus says about you in His Word instead." Amen.

In the next chapter, we'll move from the supernatural to spiritual warfare. You'll have to engage principalities and powers if you want to see revival in our region.

9

Engaging Principalities and Powers

Every region is home to principalities, powers, and various spiritual rulers that work to keep people in bondage—and actively resist the establishment of revival hubs. Although entire volumes have been penned on the topic of spiritual warfare—and we won't rehash the basics of battle in this chapter—it is worth calling out specific spirits that come against revival hubs and offering some strategies to stand and withstand.

God places strategic voices and mantles in specific territories to establish truth, breakthrough and blessing. There is supernatural favor upon the voices that God sends. Of course, there is also supernatural resistance to those voices. The enemy understands that if he can silence particular voices in a territory then he can stop the work of transformation. Religion and Jezebel are two prime enemies against revival.

Think about it for a minute. A believer who attends church year-after-year but never gets spiritually equipped, activated and sent is no threat to the enemy. Instead, the devil fights equipping voices of transformation hoping to diminish their impact. He fights the proclamation of truth. He fights the establishment of faith. He fights the flow of power and anointing! Jezebel's mission is to silence these voices and run them out of the territory so the devil can maintain his grip. He loves to partner with religion and lukewarm voices that will bow to the demonic ruler over the territory.

Apostolic and prophetic gifts expose and confront principalities and powers in a territory. Although each territory may have different spirits operating, there is a common ground in revival realms. Stand your ground! Keep declaring truth. Keep speaking the messages that burn in your belly. Don't allow discouragement to stop you. Be the voice that God has called you to be. Pray for the voices of transformation in your region. Form a prayer covering that strengthens them in the work they are called to do. Together, we shall reap the harvest.

Dismantling Lies

Revival-minded people in the new move of God will dig wells and establish revival hubs, ultimately bringing awakening and enduring transformation. Part of this process, though, is dismantling the lies of the enemy over a people and region. The enemy has erected specific strongholds in specific cities. You can often see those strongholds manifest in the thinking and actions of the people who live there.

Here are some practical examples: Las Vegas has a gambling influence while San Francisco has a homosexual influence and New York has a Babylonian influence. That influence can impact the way people think. Apostolic and prophetic ministries join forces to identify these strongholds—which aren't always as blatant as the ones in our examples—and work to displace them so the King of

Glory can reign.

You'll find one consistent pattern: spirits of religion and Jezebel stand hard against revival in any city where people are co-laboring with Christ to light a fire. Apostolic and prophetic gifts do not shrink back from the battle, but rally God's people against the enemy to tear down his throne and advance the Kingdom of God in a territory.

If you are going to contend for revival in your territory, you'll have to do more than pray. You'll have to take up your armor and fight. Paul the apostle explains:

"Put on the whole armor of God that you may be able to stand against the schemes of the devil. For our fight is not against flesh and blood, but against principalities, against powers, against the rulers of the darkness of this world, and against spiritual forces of evil in the heavenly places. Therefore take up the whole armor of God that you may be able to resist in the evil day, and having done all, to stand" (Ephesians 6:11-13).

In this emerging move of God, we need the David mantle—we need the release of worshipping warriors. Those carrying a mantle like David—a fresh anointing, a prophetic spirit, worship that has been birthed in the secret place—are being brought forth in this hour with powerful arrows of deliverance in their hands to destroy the works of the enemy. It is time to tear down strongholds the enemy has established to hold back the move of God and His glory. There is a David generation arising that will press into the holy place with fresh prophetic sounds, unashamed worship and a warrior heart!

The David mantle brings freedom, renewed vision and yoke-destroying power as fresh fire pours forth. Despite persecution from other religious leaders in the area, people with a David mantle understand this spiritual warfare reality: "For the weapons of our warfare are not carnal, but mighty through God to the pulling down of strongholds, casting down imaginations and every high thing that exalts itself against the knowledge of God, bringing every thought into captivity to the obedience of Christ, and being ready to punish all disobedience when your obedience is complete" (2 Corinthians 10:4-6).

THREE ATTACKS TO GUARD AGAINST

As you set out to establish your revival hub—or continue fanning the flames of revival in your hub—you'll consistently discover there are three key attacks against you: religious voices; agents of false fire; and controlling powers. Let's take a brief look at each one.

Religious voices value power and comfort above the move of God. They want the fruit of the new move while clinging to the comfort of the old way. This spirit will stop the flow and ultimately drain the power of God. Jesus said of the religious rulers in His day: "Woe to you, scribes and Pharisees, hypocrites! You are like whitewashed tombs, which indeed appear beautiful outwardly, but inside are full of dead men's bones and of all uncleanness" (Matthew 23:27). And He said plenty more about the religious spirit, which makes the Word of God of no effect through tradition, effectively killing off the supernatural power of God.

Next, agents of false fire will attempt to pollute the purity of the move of God. These are people who have opened the door to false power and wrong spiritual influence. They can be set free but you must not give the false fire they carry any measure of authority. Sooner or later, God always puts out the strange fire, though not in such dramatic fashion as we see in Leviticus 10:1-3 because of His grace:

"Now Nadab and Abihu, the sons of Aaron, each took his censer and put fire in it, and put incense on it, and offered strange fire before the Lord, which He did not command them to do. Then a fire came out from the Lord and devoured them, and they died before the Lord. Then Moses said to Aaron, 'This is what the Lord spoke, saying: 'I will be sanctified by those who come near Me; and before all the people I will be glorified.' And Aaron held his peace."

Controlling powers want to stop the flow through a controlling spirit. Although Jezebel is not essentially a spirit of control—it's a seducing spirit that leads God's servants into immorality and idolatry according to Revelation 2:10—control is a key manifestation of the Jezebel spirit. You can read more about that in my (Jennifer's) books *The Spiritual Warrior's Guide to Defeating Jezebel* and *Satan's Deadly Trio*, which addresses how Jezebel, witchcraft and religion work together. People who have yielded to a controlling spirit will be attracted to transformation ministries. They come in with the right words and a seemingly spiritual attitude yet their motive is not to serve but to control—to cut off the revival.

The key to victory over these enemies is sticking to the vision of transformation. Love all people that God sends but use wisdom in leading and be aware that the enemy will fight your mandate in various ways. God wants to partner with radical agents of change to birth life-giving ministries in regions of the earth whose mark is revival, awakening and transformation.

Contending With the Saul Spirit

We honor the men and women—generals of God—who have been laboring for revival for decades. Many intercessors have been contending in prayer for the next great move of God long before we knew the Lord. Many have experienced moves of God, like the Voice of Healing movement or the Charismatic movement. We are intentional about honoring them and gleaning wisdom from them.

As we've said before, many times when a new move of God erupts the greatest critics are those who led and participated in the previous move of God. Here's why: It typically sounds, looks and functions differently than the previous move. When the new erupts it challenges hearts to move into another Holy Spirit dimension. Each move builds upon the previous one. Revival is a progressive journey. There is no stopping point until we arrive in heaven.

You may have to contend with a Saul spirit along the way. During his reign as King, Saul was transformed from a meek, passionate lover of God to a domineering, oppressive ruler who actively fought against those whom God was raising up. David was a powerful young prophet who found his identity in the presence of God. Saul at first welcomed but later resisted the emerging ministry of David because of jealousy. Look at the transition from 1 Samuel 18:5-12:

"David went out wherever Saul sent him, and he was successful. So Saul set him over the men of war, and it was pleasing in the sight of all the people and also in the sight of the servants of Saul. When they came home, as David was returning from slaying the Philistine, the women came out from all cities of Israel to meet King Saul, singing and dancing, with tambourines, with joy, and with musical instruments. The dancing women sang and said, 'Saul has slain his thousands, and David his ten thousands.'

"Saul became very angry, and this saying was displeasing to him. Therefore he said, 'They have ascribed to David ten thousands, but to me they have ascribed thousands. Now what remains for him to have but the kingdom?' So Saul was suspicious of David from that day and forward. It came to pass the following day, that an evil spirit from God came upon Saul, so that he raved in the midst of the house. And David was playing the lyre, as at other times. Now there was a spear in Saul's hand. And Saul threw the spear. For he said, 'I will pin David to the wall.' But David avoided him two times. Saul was afraid of David because the Lord was with him but had departed from Saul."

Saul was tormented by inner turmoil and raging insecurity. An insecure leader often becomes a controlling leader. Revival hubs will not be led by Sauls. A Saul cannot usher in the fresh prophetic anointing that will slay the giant and bring the victory. Only a David can bring the necessary components because he or she has been formed in the secret place. "Davids" desire presence more than platform. "Davids" live for the secret place. "Davids" have prevailed in secret and will be rewarded openly.

Saul fought against the next generation of great leaders. A person dwelling in the house of Saul controls, binds and restricts! They do not embrace fresh moves of God but view everything through a lens of personal pride. This mentality will not be effective in the move that God is birthing in the land.

There is a washing and cleansing taking place. Leaders are being invited to cross over into a fresh move of God. God is no respecter of persons (see Acts 10:34). He is calling the hungry forth! The Father is wooing His children to come up higher with Him. At the same time, there is a radical new breed arising of every age, race and background that are willing to dig the wells—and engage the principalities and powers—to release the rivers!

And it takes a team. In the next chapter, we'll explore how team ministry releases synergies.

10

TEAM MINISTRY RELEASES SYNERGIES

Team ministry synergies are at the core of healthy revival hubs. Mature revival hubs will see the entire five-fold ministry—apostles, prophets, evangelists, pastors and teachers—in operation. And not only in operation, but functioning and flowing together; honoring one another; leading teams and ultimately raising up strong believers who can operate in the manifold grace of God.

Teamwork is vital to ministry in this hour. The truth is, teamwork has always been vital to ministry in God's paradigm but the church has slipped into a one-man-only model that leaves most believers sitting on the bench as spectators. Whether in the Old Testament or the New Testament, you'll find that God places value on teamwork. As it's been said, teamwork makes the dream work.

Think about it for a minute. Moses shared leadership with Aaron and Miriam and eventually 70 others he anointed for the work of the ministry. Nehemiah worked teams, each with specific assignments, to rebuild Jerusalem. David had a band of mighty men who partnered with him. Jesus sent out His disciples two by two (Luke 10:1). And you won't find Paul flying solo in his revival adventures. Paul completed his assignments with an apostolic company. The

Lord gave me (Ryan) a prophetic word about this reemerging model:

"I am calling forth the apostolic companies who will go forth and occupy the territory. They will be sent forth arm-in-arm, hand-in-hand, linked by My Spirit. I am raising up divine ministry relationships and partnerships in the earth. There is a paradigm of traveling ministry that will be modeled in this season that is a return to the model in the early church. I will send forth apostolic companies to see, proclaim, release, impart, revive and equip.

"This assignment will require much grace. There must be a death to personal agendas. The focus must be on the Kingdom plans for people, ministries, cities, nations and regions. I will send forth the apostles and prophets linked together by common purpose and destiny. They will go on Kingdom assignments. I am nudging the hearts of many right now in the secret place.

"I am awakening them to see the model of revival in the book of Acts and the power of team ministry. This is not something that can be fulfilled by natural desire or understanding. It must be a work of My Spirit. Competition must bow; pride must bow; old religious mindsets must bow. For those that have cried out to me for their region have moved my heart. I desire to raise up the apostolic companies and send them forth to the regions."

Modern-day ministry teams of apostles, prophets, evangelists, pastors and teachers will have a tremendous impact on the spiritual condition of a church. When Jesus came and ministered He gathered a team around Him. He ordained 12 to be with Him. Jesus established the team concept and left a pattern for New Testament ministry. In order to fully reestablish this concept, we must break the religious concept of pastor as priest: marrying, burying, counseling, preaching, leading and being a one-man ministry.

The Apostolic Pioneering Mandate

You can describe the apostolic anointing in many ways—it fathers, builds, governs, and much more—but pioneering is one aspect of the apostolic that the Lord is emphasizing as we press in to take back what the enemy stole (or perhaps better put, what we gave up) in our regions. Merriam-Webster defines pioneer as "a person who helps create or develop new ideas, methods, etc.; someone who is one of the first people to move to and live in a new area."

Apostolic pioneers go to unknown places to build, occupy and establish new paradigms, which are not really new paradigms but rather the restoration of God's patterns and plans. Apostles are set in the church first by God (see 1 Corinthians 12:28). "First" in this verse is the Greek work "proton," meaning "first in time, order, or rank. This choice of language paints a picture of a spiritual pioneer who goes out ahead." Just as the pioneers in early America ventured into unknown territory to lay claim to lands, people with an apostolic anointing move into the unknown and stake a claim on a territory by the authority of the Spirit of God.

Apostolic pioneers first hear, see or otherwise recognize a call to action, then must discern to whom or where God is sending them. It's not an exact science. At times, when Paul and his apostolic team went through certain cities to preach the Word the Holy Spirit stopped him in favor of a more strategic mission (see Acts 16:6-10). Paul concluded that the Lord wanted him to preach the gospel in Macedonia only after the Holy Spirit twice prevented him from preaching in other cities, then gave him a vision that clearly laid out the next leg of his missionary journey. In other words, Paul had his plans but the Holy Spirit had different plans. This is one of the key reasons why it's so vital for the apostles and prophets to run together.

And we know that the church—and revival hubs—are built on the foundation of apostles and prophets, Christ Jesus Himself being the corner stone (see Ephesians 2:20).

Apostles are hard-wired for mission and mandate. Sometimes they act out of a supernatural encounter, like Moses at the burning bush (see Exodus 3:7-10) or Paul on the road to Damascus (see Acts 9). Other times they operate out of conviction, like Nehemiah when he set out to rebuild Jerusalem: "Finally, I said to them, 'You see the distress that we are in, how Jerusalem is devastated and its gates are burned with fire. Come, and let us rebuild the wall of Jerusalem so that we will no more be a reproach.' Then I told them that the hand of my God had been good to me and also about the king's words that he had spoken to me. And they said, 'Let us rise up and build!' So they strengthened their hands for the good work" (Nehemiah 2:17-19).

THE APOSTOLIC TEAM PARADIGM

The apostolic paradigm is a team paradigm. As spiritual fathers (and mothers) apostles establish and lead spiritual families. An apostolic team, then, is a group of ministry gifts and individuals sent forth with a united cause and specific mandate and mission from the Lord. Apostles develop and establish teams with a gift and personality mix that matches the mission. An apostolic team for one assignment may look different than an apostolic team for another assignment.

Consider this scene from Acts 11:25-26: "Then Barnabas went to Tarsus to look for Saul. When he had found him, he brought him to Antioch. For a whole year they met with the church and taught a considerable crowd. And the disciples were first called Christians in Antioch." Barnabas was working to advance a growing move God that Paul was also working to pioneer. When they finally connected, the Bible says they ministered as a team in Antioch. So we see the team concept of New Testament ministry established firmly in Scripture.

After Barnabas came to Antioch he went to Tarsus to get Paul (then Saul) in order to build and advance the growing move of God. Barnabas and Paul assembled themselves with the church at Antioch and ministered in a team capacity. They established the team concept at Antioch. Barnabas and Saul were then commissioned from that place to take financial relief to Christians in Judea (see Acts 11:29). We see the apostolic return to the revival hub—their home base—at Antioch again (see Acts 12:25) and then getting sent out again (see Acts 13).

DEVELOPING APOSTOLIC COMPANIES

Apostolic teams can be as small as two people, like Barnabas and Saul, but as the team grows it becomes a fully operating apostolic company, or group of people. The U.S. military uses the word "company" to describe a unit of soldiers. Teams are good for traveling ministry assignments but you ultimately need a company—a unit of soldiers—to occupy the territory and release the Kingdom in a region.

A team is like a strike force going forth with a specific objective. Typically, a team takes on a short-term assignment. By contrast, a company is an occupying force that enters a territory with a long-term call, mission and strategy. An apostolic ministry will often appoint various teams under the direction of the primary apostle involved. The apostle may or may not be on site but offers spiritual backup and prayer.

Sometimes both an apostolic team and company are needed

to bring the shift that is required. The team is made up of those carrying the message by the breath of God and the company is there to reinforce that message," says Greg Crawford, an apostolic leader who pioneered The Base in Des Moines, Iowa. "Generally the team has seasoned five-fold people that are also seasoned in the message. The company will be those who have been impacted by the message and are possibly future leaders. All apostolic teams are part of the company but not all the company is part of an apostolic team due to overall calling and grace function."

Jesus formed an apostolic company and sent them forth: "Then He called His twelve disciples together and gave them power and authority over all demons and to cure diseases. And He sent them to preach the kingdom of God and to heal the sick" (Luke 9:1-2).

A company is not just five-fold ministry gifts but a people sent to a region to establish the Kingdom of God and bring supernatural manifestations that spark revival in the hearts of people. Of course, this breaks the religious paradigm that operates based on felt needs (which we spoke about in an earlier chapter) so there will be resistance. If you are going to serve on an apostolic company of revivalists looking to break the power of religion that has rocked the church to sleep, you can expect persecution. In 2 Corinthians 11:24-28, Paul wrote:

"Five times I received from the Jews forty lashes minus one. Three times I was beaten with rods; once I was stoned; three times I suffered shipwreck; a night and a day I have been in the deep; in journeys often, in perils of waters, in perils of robbers, in perils by my own countrymen, in perils by the Gentiles, in perils in the city, in perils in the wilderness, in perils in the sea, in perils among false brothers; in weariness and painfulness, in sleeplessness often, in hunger and thirst, in fastings often, and in cold and nakedness. Beside the external things, the care of all the churches pressures me daily."

REVIVAL-MINDED PROPHETS EMERGE

Apostolic companies need prophets. Where would the body of Christ be without prophets? It would be incomplete with no hope of ever fully maturing. Jesus gave equipping gifts to His Church to help Christians grow up and unify to build a holy temple where the Spirit of God feels at home. Removing even one of those five factors (graces) out of the spiritual equation results in an erroneous solution to the challenges facing the Church.

Prophets are spiritually equipped to serve as the eyes, ears and voice to the body of Christ. Although prophets have many functions, one of the most vital in this hour from an awakening perspective is the John the Baptist mandate to lead the church into repentance—to prepare a people for the Second Coming of the Lord. Matthew 3:1-6 says:

"In those days John the Baptist came, preaching in the wilderness of Judea, and saying, 'Repent, for the kingdom of heaven is at hand.' For this is he who was spoken of by the prophet Isaiah, saying: 'The voice of one crying in the wilderness: 'Prepare the way of the Lord; make His paths straight.' This same John had clothing made of camel's hair, a leather belt around his waist, and his food was locusts and wild honey. Then Jerusalem, and all Judea, and all the region around the Jordan went out to him, and were baptized by him in the Jordan, confessing their sins."

There is no revival without repentance—and it's not just repentance from sins like lying, gossiping, and prayerlessness. It's a change in the way we think about church, the gifts of the Spirit, and even Jesus Himself. The spirits of religion and Jezebel that killed the prophets in the old days are still working to silence the voices of the prophets today. These spirits have watered down the gospel, shut out—or perverted—the gifts of the spirit, and skewed our perspective of Jesus as Bridegroom, King and Judge.

Meanwhile, some prophets in this hour are prophesying judgment and curses—doom and gloom. Clearly, God has lifted some of His hedge of protection from America and other nations, but using our anointed mouths to continually confess judgment over mercy will bear fruit we don't want to eat. When God wanted to judge Sodom and Gomorrah, Abraham interceded for these cities (see Genesis 18-19). When God wanted to destroy Israel, Moses interceded for a rebellious people (see Exodus 32). And Jonah warned of the coming wrath of God and the people repented and stayed off the judgment (see Jonah 3).

God is a God of hope and in this emerging move of God, as prophets set out as individuals, in teams or in companies, they need to be sober-minded and warn of the wages of sin and the law of sowing and reaping sin, but the prophetic voices most closely aligned with God's heart in this hour are carrying a message of hope against hope.

It's not too late for America or whatever nation you are in. 2 Chronicles 7:14 is still true. But let's pull back and read that Scripture in context. The context is that Solomon just finished building a house for the Lord. Catch that. As revivalists, we're laboring first and foremost build a habitation for the Lord—revival hubs filled with His glory—from which we send out apostolic teams and companies to establish the Kingdom of God. Let's look at the Scripture:

"Then the Lord appeared to Solomon at night, and He said to

Solomon, 'I have heard your prayer, and I have chosen for Myself in this place a house of sacrifice. When I shut up the heaven and there is no rain, or when I command the locusts to devour the land, or send pestilence on My people, if My people, who are called by My name, will humble themselves and pray, and seek My face and turn from their wicked ways, then I will hear from heaven, and will forgive their sin and will heal their land. Now My eyes will be open and My ears attentive to the prayer of this place. So now I have chosen and consecrated this house that My name be there continually. My eyes and heart will be there for all days" (2 Chronicles 7:12-16).

When we build a revival hub God's way and stand in the gap, repenting for the sins of our nation, He will hear from heaven, forgive our sin and heal our land. (We'll talk more about this in the chapter on transformation.) His ears will be attentive to the prayers in that place and it will be a place consecrated for His purposes where people can hear His heartbeat. For all the many functions of prophetic ministry in this hour, leading people into repentance is perhaps the largest key to transforming revival.

EVERY APOSTOLIC COMPANY NEEDS EVANGELISTS AND PASTORS

Evangelists are vital to what God wants to do in this hour. An evangelist is one whose vocation or calling is to preach the gospel; the good news of Jesus Christ. You can no more keep an evangelist from preaching the gospel than you can keep a doctor from practicing medicine in an emergency.

Although all believers are called to do the work of an evangelist, sharing the good tidings is part of the five-fold evangelist's spiritual DNA. Of course, evangelists are also called to spread the passion for soul-winning by equipping believers how to share the gospel effectively. Evangelists are key to the next great move of God. Greg Laurie, dubbed the "evangelist of the future" by Billy Graham, put it this way:

"The secular culture doesn't need revival; they need evangelism. And here is the interesting thing: Evangelism doesn't necessarily produce revival, but revival always produces evangelism. Whenever there has been an awakening, there has been an evangelistic thrust that has come as a result. When God's people are awakened, when they are restored, when they are revived, then they go out and start doing what they should have been doing all along, which is proclaiming the gospel. I pray that the church will have a revival. And I pray that our culture will hear the gospel."

Charles Finney, a leader in the Second Great Awakening, said revival had two purposes: to revive the church and to win the lost. The evangelist has a role to play in both scenarios. The evangelist not only preaches the gospel to sinners, but also preaches revival to wake up the church. Some evangelists are full-blown revivalists, like our friend Joe Joe Dawson, president of Burn Texarkana.

"How many times have you heard the word 'revival' in the church over the past 30 years? Some churches pray for revival while other churches plan a four-day revival. America needs a revival or a Third Great Awakening to come soon," says Dawson, our co-laborer on the New Breed Revival Network. "So many people ask me how can the church of America, the church of today have a great visitation for the Holy Spirit. I always simply reply that the recipe for revival is in the Bible!"

Once a lost soul comes to know the Lord, the evangelist's job is done. Now, they need a pastor to love on them and comfort them. Pastors are shepherds anointed by God to take care of the sheep (believers). If there is an explosion of momentum in the church there must be an explosion of pastoral grace and ministry! Yet, it is important to note that planting is not a pastoral function but an apostolic one. We don't see any New Testament churches planted by pastors yet pastors are vital to revival hubs.

So what is the pastor's role in a revival hub? Pastor John Kilpatrick, a key figure in the Brownsville Revival, says this: "When people come to church, pastors often don't really realize we determine what's put on the table. A pastor is like a nursing mother. Whatever that mother eats is what that baby gets through the breast. And whatever that pastor believes, whatever he's passionate about, whatever he has studied is exactly in a different form what the congregation will receive."

The pastor's role, then, is to seek personal revival, to cultivate a personal hunger and desperation for God, to seek to please the Lord instead of man, to host the presence of God in worship services, and to otherwise serve as an example to the flock. Then when revival hits, the pastor must be a good steward of the revival and a shepherd to the new souls that are coming into the kingdom.

"I went on a desperate journey mainly just to connect. It wasn't for my ministry. It was for me. I wasn't even thinking about ministry. I was just thinking about for me. Personally, I have to do this. And if nobody else wants me to, then that's too bad. If I lose the church over it, I'm still going to go for it," says Pastor Steve Grey, who led the Smithton Outpouring in 1996 and the Kansas City Revival from 2008-2011.

"I had all that determined ahead of time. I wasn't making up my mind as it was coming at me or as it was happening. I'd already made up my mind. That helped me because I had no battle to fight. All the battles were fought before the first event ever happened. One mistake people make is that they are just journeying to see if something will happen. Then, of course, comes tons of prayer. You pour your soul out."

THE RESURGENCE OF TEACHERS

Last but not least, teachers are vital to revival hubs and the emerging move of God.

The teaching ministry establishes right belief systems, strong foundations, renews the corporate mindset and steers believers away from deception. Bible-based teaching is absolutely critical in this hour with the strong delusion that's infiltrating the church.

Yes, we need fresh wind and intense fire. Yes, we need a powerful movement of revival and outpouring. Yes, we need miracles, signs and wonders. But we also need strong teaching to establish right believing. We must recognize the need for the teacher's office in revival hubs. We must embrace and release the teachers to bring forth truth. In fact, we believe that the teaching ministry will give birth to sustainable moves of God.

Teachers have massive responsibilities in the Kingdom of God. Consider the sobering words of James, the apostle of practical faith: "My brothers, not many of you should become teachers, knowing that we shall receive the greater judgment" (James 3:1-5). Why will teachers receive the greater judgment? The context in which this verse appears connects to the words of the mouth. The words teachers speak impact the minds of believers. The Bible speaks of false teachers whose teaching is not sound but tickles ears of those who don't love the truth (2 Timothy 4:3-4). Peter also warns about false teachers who bring in destructive heresies, even denying the

Master who brought them (2 Peter 2:1).

Right after James explains that teachers shall receive the greater judgment, he explains that: "We all err in many ways. But if any man does not err in word, he is a perfect man and able also to control the whole body. See how we put bits in the mouths of horses that they may obey us, and we control their whole bodies. And observe ships. Though they are so great and are driven by fierce winds, yet they are directed with a very small rudder wherever the captain pleases. Even so, the tongue is a little part of the body and boasts great things. See how great a forest a little fire kindles" (James 3:2-5).

The bottom line is teachers affect the belief systems of those who listen—and this poor influence can spread far and wide. YouTube is full of Christian teachers whose doctrine does not line up with the Word of God. As this emerging move of God comes forward to birth outpouring, awakening and transformation the belief systems of individual believers are critically important.

Under the New Covenant we have been released from earning righteousness based on keeping law and brought into righteousness by faith through grace. Our faith is the direct result of what we believe. Belief systems are formed through line upon line teaching. This is why the Apostle Paul would take time to identify wrong teaching in his churches—and judge it as false. He understood that teaching forms a belief system and that belief system either builds or hinders faith, which ultimately dictates how much of the promise a believer walks in.

In this move of God believers are going to be revived and equipped. Revival hubs are springing up with a transformation mandate. Believers must come into their full identity with no hindrances. They must know, understand and activate the power of God in their lives so that they can be a Kingdom connection, releasing God's power to others. False teaching and wrong believing will block the flow. We see teachers locked arm-in-arm with apostles advancing truth that leads to transformation, first of minds, then of bodies of believers, then of cities and regions.

We pray the Holy Spirit breathes a fresh north wind upon the teaching ministry in this hour. We pray that the scrolls of heaven unfold, revealing the mysteries of God to be communicated with His children. We pray those who have been teaching for years rise up under a fresh wind and many more heed the call to teach God's people, feed His sheep and release manna. We pray dry teaching services will yield to life-giving rivers of revelation flowing unhindered in Jesus' name.

EVERY BELIEVER NEEDS APOSTOLIC GRIT

Maybe you are not called as part of the five-fold. That doesn't mean there's not a place in the apostolic company for you. We need every revival-minded believer to join together in unity and press in for a Third Great Awakening, and then sustain an awakened life. You'll need apostolic grit to press into your revivalist calling.

The apostolic grace is an enduring grace and apostolic living is a life of endurance. We endure spiritual attacks. We endure hard truths. We endure growing pains. We endure, endure and endure some more. And we have the grit necessary to do it. The apostolic brings with it an endurance-boosting grace that will carry you through the most trying times if you follow the Spirit of God. Brother Webster calls this inner grit a "firmness of mind and spirit, an unyielding courage in the face of hardship or danger."

Excuses are your enemy and in the Church of Jesus Christ there is no such thing as instant grit. When things get tough and you want to give up, read Apostle Paul's second letter to Timothy and the sage advice it contains to a young believer embracing a great move of God: "When the going gets rough, take it on the chin with the rest of us, the way Jesus did. A soldier on duty doesn't get caught up in making deals at the marketplace. He concentrates on carrying out orders. An athlete who refuses to play by the rules will never get anywhere. It's the diligent farmer who gets the product. Think it over. God will make it all plain" (2 Timothy 2:3-7 MSG).

In the next chapter, we'll talk about digging the wells and building the walls.

11

DIGGING REGIONAL WELLS

A revival hub is a ministry center that pushes, prays, prophesies and ultimately contends to be a regional well. Keep in mind that a well is much different from an outpouring, but as revival-minded people we must embrace both concepts. Let's dive into the differences.

An outpouring is a supernatural move of the Holy Spirit that emphasizes a particular gift or ministry. Over the generations, there have been healing outpourings, fire outpourings, charismatic gift outpourings, glory outpourings, and so on. An outpouring typically has a destined beginning and end. It is seasonal—even if the season is many years—and has a specific purpose in the earth. The Holy Spirit pours out what is needed in the hour or in a generation.

Revival hubs, then, may have many glorious outpourings but revival hubs are called to do more than prepare for an outpouring— they are called to dig a deep well in a region. Even by its natural definition, an outpouring is different than a well. An outpouring is a pouring out of something from above. A well issues water from the earth. You don't dig for an outpouring. You receive it freely. A well has to be dug before it will bring forth water or oil.

A revival well is a spiritual well that releases a constant supply of personal awakening, radical outpourings of glory, healing and miracles, deliverance, radical worship, powerful prophetic flows, salvation and full throttle Kingdom ministry. A revival well will spring forth in a territory as the members of the hub press in. The well must be dug, unlocked and maintained.

THE ISAAC MANDATE

In Isaac's day, there was a famine in the land. Sounds sort of like today—only it's not natural food but spiritual food. Indeed, there's a Word famine in the land. People are starving for the pure Word of God whether they know it or not. In Isaac's case, the Lord warned him not to go down to Egypt but pointed him to Gerar, where he sowed in the land and reaped a hundred fold in the same year! He became so prosperous that King Abimelek sent him away. Isaac had to pioneer in a new territory—and he had to redig some wells.

"Isaac dug again the wells of water, which they had dug in the days of Abraham his father, for the Philistines had stopped them up after the death of Abraham. He called their names after the names his father had called them" (Genesis 26:18).

This is significant. Isaac returned to the places his father, Abraham, had dug. He knew there was a stream of life there and sought out to uncap those wells. We need to have the same mind as Isaac in this regard—to take on the mandate to uncap the wells from previous generations. Those wells are rich with miracles, signs and wonders. Those wells are rich with revelation. Those wells are rich with glory. But it's going to take some labor in the spirit and in the natural to get the job done.

Think about digging for a minute. Have you ever taken a shovel and really had to dig in hot weather and hard ground? It takes a lot of effort. You have to physically plunge the metal shovel into the ground, then lift the dirt out and move it. (And you need the right shovel, but that's a different teaching.) It can be exhausting even for the most physically fit person.

Now consider what you are digging through. In the Bible, dirt represents humanity. When God created mankind what did He form us out of? The dust (dirt) of the earth. What was blocking up the old wells? Dirt! What had to be moved out of the way in order to get the flow going? Dirt, dust—flesh!

Indeed, our own flesh will oftentimes oppose the release of a powerful revival well. The natural opinions of men can stand in stark opposition to the move of God. Revival cuts through programs, carnal thinking and self-reliance. A revival culture is one that is deeply dependent upon God and His glory. The enemy will often pull on the appetites and thoughts of carnal people to create division and plug the wells. Paul the apostle put it this way:

"I say then, walk in the Spirit, and you shall not fulfill the lust of the flesh. For the flesh lusts against the Spirit, and the Spirit against the flesh. These are in opposition to one another, so that you may not do the things that you please. But if you are led by the Spirit, you are not under the law.

"Now the works of the flesh are revealed, which are these: adultery, sexual immorality, impurity, lewdness, idolatry, sorcery, hatred, strife, jealousy, rage, selfishness, dissensions, heresies, envy, murders, drunkenness, carousing, and the like. I warn you, as I previously warned you, that those who do such things shall not inherit the kingdom of God. But the fruit of the Spirit is love, joy, peace, patience, gentleness, goodness, faith, meekness, and self-control; against such there is no law. Those who are Christ's have crucified the flesh with its passions and lusts" (Galatians 5:16-24).

WARRING REGIONAL DEMONS

Again, the Philistines—an enemy of God's people—had intentionally plugged the wells. Not only do we need to get flesh out of the way in order to dig a revival well, we also have to engage in a spiritual fight against principalities and powers. We talk more about this in Chapter 9. Suffice it to say that regional demons have long held onto the hearts and minds of people. They will not simply roll over and go away. We have to fight the good fight of faith and enter the wrestling ring to contend for revival.

With that in mind, a revival hub must be a place of strategic transformation, clarity—and battle. Digging a regional well will require boldness, commitment and tenacity. This is why the apostolic spirit is a vital component of a revival hub. Apostles are generals in God's army. They have a grace to release strategy, advance the vision and take down the enemy. Of course, prophets must be right alongside apostles providing divine insight. It is often prophets in a region that identify the type of enemy, which empowers the apostle to create spiritual strategy and march the Ekklesia on to victory.

As he sought to redig the wells Abraham established, Isaac honored the labor of the previous generation. He would not have been successful if he had not moved in honor. To be sure, a generational divide is one common attack against the next great move of God. This is purely demonic.

Fathers of the generations before us have dug wells that we can tap into to advance revival and awakening in our generation—but we must honor them despite any downfalls we discern. The healing generals of the previous generations dug strong miracle wells and the carnality of the present day church culture clogged them up— but we can unplug them and release a powerful healing move for this hour! It is the former and the latter rain coming together. There is an unlocking of ancient wells along with the discovery of new ones destined for this generation. There is an inheritance blessing available.

By the same token, some of the current generals are refusing to honor what God is doing in this hour. It's common for leaders of the last great move of God to attack, downgrade or merely fail to acknowledge the next great move of God. As we've mentioned in this book, a Saul spirit can rise up in otherwise fine men and women of God to kill next-generation pioneers. The spirit of religion is murderous. The spirit of Jezebel wants to cut off the voice of God. There is always a war for revival. No matter how long we've been walking with the Lord or how many moves of God we've experienced, we need to intentionally honor our brothers and sisters in Christ who walked before us, who are walking with us, and who are coming up behind us.

WELLS OF IMPARTATION AND ACTIVATION

We're working on another book about redigging the wells of revival where we will go into greater detail about strategies and tactics. In the context of our revival hubs vision, we'll focus more narrowly on how revival hubs fit into the regional revival well mandate. Although the concept of digging suggests hard work, for example, divine revelation ultimately establishes regional wells for the purpose of fueling a move of God and activating the work of the kingdom.

We spent all of chapter 3 comparing revival hubs and church

models. But we'd like to reemphasize one point in this discussion about regional revival wells. One of the primary differences between a revival hub and a traditional church mindset is the territorial mandate. Most traditional local churches are primarily focused on the growth and maintenance of their own body. A revival hub has a Kingdom mandate that is focused on Kingdom equipping and exploits within a region. That thrust requires the Ephesians 4:11-14 reality of equipping the saints for the work of the ministry.

Indeed, part of the revival hub's DNA is impartation and activation. Paul the apostle understood the power of impartation and he shares the revelation in Scripture. Impartation is a transfer of divine grace, power and ability. To the church in Rome, he said, "For I long to see you, that I may impart to you some spiritual gift, so that you may be strengthened" (Romans 1:11). Paul was eagerly anticipating visiting the believers in Rome. What was his focus? It was impartation. He wanted to make a spiritual deposit.

But that's not the only example. Paul also exhorted Timothy twice to tap into the gift that he received through impartation. Paul reminded him to "stir up the gift of God, which is in you by the laying on of my hands" (see 2 Timothy 1:6) and not to "neglect that gift that is in you, which was given to you by prophecy, with the laying on of hands by the elders" (1 Timothy 4:14). This is not merely a New Testament idea. It's a God idea. Moses imparted a prophetic spirit to 70 elders (see Numbers 11:16-17) and Jesus sent out 72 with authority to heal the sick and cast out devils (Luke 10).

Revival hubs leaders impart to spiritual sons and daughters according to the will of God—and activate them into their calling. A healthy revival hub, then, is not only a gathering place but also an empowering place. Although empowering can take place in many ways, impartation is a vital key to a spiritual exchange. There must be a deliberate focus on the release of gifts and anointing. People must be trained to draw these gifts out of the leadership team and also visiting speakers.

Beyond impartation is activation. Merriam-Webster defines "activate" as "to make (as molecules) reactive or more reactive" or "to start working or cause to start working." Just as we touch a screen to activate a system or touch a button to activate a camera, we can touch (lay hands) on someone by the unction of the Spirit of God and activate the gift inside them so it will "start working." Of course, impartation and activation are just the beginning. Equipping and training must follow to fulfill the Ephesians 4:11-14 reality:

"He gave some to be apostles, prophets, evangelists, pastors, and teachers, for the equipping of the saints, for the work of service, and for the building up of the body of Christ, until we all come into the unity of the faith and of the knowledge of the Son of God, into a complete man, to the measure of the stature of the fullness of Christ, so we may no longer be children, tossed here and there by waves and carried about with every wind of doctrine by the trickery of men, by craftiness with deceitful scheming."

EMBRACING OUTSIDE REINFORCEMENTS

Each revival hub will have a general or generals positioned in the region by the hand of God—but they must recognize the need for outside reinforcements. Merriam-Webster defines "reinforce" as to strengthen (a group of people) with new supplies or more people; to strengthen (something, such as clothing or a building) by adding more material for support, and; to encourage or give support to (an idea, behavior, feeling, etc.).

Reinforcement is also a military term. Always remember that you are in a spiritual war. In this context, reinforcement is a military operation (often involving new supplies of men or material) to strengthen a military force or aid in the performance of its mission, according to Vocabulary.com. That means a revival hub is a place that welcomes key voices and gifts into a region in order to make divine deposits that lead to activation and ultimately transformation. Revival hub leaders must be very intentional about hosting conferences, training seminars and inviting the right gifts to supplement where there is a lack in the particular region.

In summary, as you set out to dig a regional well, understand that the assignment is not just to a local body of believers—it is to a territory. Establish strong apostolic and prophetic prayer ministry to govern and shift the spiritual climate in the region and release prophetic direction. Build a stable foundation through strong teaching. Press. Pray. Prophesy. Release outpouring. Pursue spiritual gifts. And bring in fresh voices and ministry gifts to speak into the region and leave a lasting impartation. In the next chapter, we'll discuss how to shift spiritual climates.

12

SHIFTING SPIRITUAL CLIMATES

One thing we've learned in our travels is this: No matter what city people live in, they always say it is a hard spiritual climate with lots of big devils. Sometimes, we go into places and the spiritual climate seems as hard as bronze. Interestingly, bronze heavens are part of the curse of the law, according to Deuteronomy 28:23.

Sometimes, it seems like our prayers hit a bronze ceiling and fall back down to the earth again. Of course, we know that's not true because God hears the prayers of the righteous (see Proverbs 15:8). But prayer often feels like a heated battle when you are in a tight spiritual climate with strongholds like witchcraft and Jezebel—or Leviathan or Python or religion or whatever spirits are waging war against revival in your territory.

There's plenty of talk in the world today about climate change. That's at least somewhat prophetic. However, what we really need to work on is not global warming—it's the battle in the unseen realm that is causing the love of many to grow cold. In other words, we need to enter intercession and worship and gospel-preaching that will shift spiritual climates, touch hearts and transform regions. We need to press into the prophetic and execute apostolic strategies that will break open heard heavens.

God uses revival tribes to shift spiritual atmospheres and transform spiritual climates. If an atmosphere is developed and maintained long enough it creates a sustainable climate. A sustainable climate produces a stronghold, or way of thinking. When we create spiritual climates where the Holy Spirit feels welcome to move freely, we see people delivered from demonic strongholds as God's thoughts replace ungodly thoughts. Systems of thought create culture.

Strongholds (systems of thought) create a culture. What if we were intentional about a revival culture, a prayer culture, a healing culture, a prophetic culture? A culture in which people are encouraged in their gift and in the supernatural to hear, see and know by the spirit? That is one of the missions of revival hubs.

What is a Spiritual Climate?

Before we go any further, let's define "spiritual climates." You can make a correlation to a natural climate, but only loosely. Let's start there. Merriam-Webster defines "climate," as a region with particular weather patterns or conditions; the usual weather conditions in a particular place or region; the usual or most widespread mood or conditions in a place; the average course of condition of the weather at a place usually over a period of years as exhibited by temperature, wind velocity, and precipitation; the prevailing set of conditions (as of temperature and humidity) indoors; or the prevailing influence of environmental conditions characterizing a group or period."

Notice that regions have climates. South Florida's climate is much different from South Seattle. Climates deal with weather patterns. It's down right chilling in Alaska and hot in Texas. It's rainy in Seattle and windy in Chicago. It's dry in New Mexico and humid in Atlanta. Spiritual climates can also shift from region to region, though they don't necessarily mirror the natural climate. The spiritual temperature in Kentucky at the time of this writing is much hotter, for example, than the spiritual temperature in some other states. Natural climates include factors like wind and rain—so do spiritual climates.

Merriam-Webster also defines a climate as the most widespread mood. I believe this is where spiritual climates are manifested in the natural. The mood of the people, in other words, is often influenced by the prevailing spirits. Where the Holy Spirit rules and reigns, you'll find hope, peace, joy, love and the fruit of His Spirit manifesting. Where the spirit of religion has erected strongholds, you'll find legalistic people with ungodly ambition who murder each other with their mouths. Where the spirit of Jezebel has erected strongholds, you'll find immorality and idolatry running rampant in the society. Where the Python spirit has erected strongholds, you'll find apathy and hopelessness. These are general statements, but you get the spiritual drift.

It's important to discern the spiritual climate in which you live because it makes you more effective in shifting the climate. Although general principles of evangelism, worship and intercession will shift spiritual climates over time, understanding what has influenced your climate gives you more wisdom to stand against that which is standing against God's will and Kingdom in your territory. If it's Jezebel, for example, then you know you need to battle against immorality and idolatry.

Just as you dress appropriately for natural climates, you must be prepared to enter various spiritual climates, discerning what is operating and taking authority over those things that stand against

God's will. We need to declare and decree the opposite of the ungodliness that's manifesting rather than continually confessing the enemy's stronghold. We see a practical example of this in Mark 5:38-42 when Jesus arrived on the scene:

"He came to the house of the ruler of the synagogue, and saw the tumult, and those who wept and wailed loudly. When He came in, He said to them, 'Why make this uproar and weep? The girl is not dead, but sleeping.' They laughed at Him in ridicule. But when He had put them all out, He took the father and the mother of the girl and those who were with Him and entered where the girl was lying. He took the girl by the hand and said to her, 'Talitha cumi,' which means, 'Little girl, I say to you, arise. Immediately the girl arose and walked, for she was twelve years of age. And they were greatly astonished."

Jesus boldly announced that the little girl was not dead but asleep. How could He say such an outrageous thing? He was looking beyond the natural dimension and seeing in the spirit. When you see in the spirit you begin to declare what you see and this gives birth to a shift! As Jesus shifted the atmosphere something new was produced. Life replaced death because of the powerful shift. Revival tribes are called to bring shift in cities and regions. There are miracles, salvations and breakthroughs hanging in the balance.

THE FOUNDATION OF SPIRITUAL SHIFTS

Prayer is the foundation of all spiritual shifts. Revival tribes go after God in prayer with everything in them. They dedicate themselves to intercession out of a heart of love for God, a love for His presence, and a love for His people. Revival tribes pursue prayer, worship and praise and are passionate about the secret place—and that passionate pursuit eventually shifts the climate, first episodically and then sustainably.

We see these realities play out in a revival tribe that gathered in an Upper Room over 2,000 years ago. Indeed, the early church was birthed in a radical Holy Ghost prayer meeting that shifted the climate. They gathered in the upper room seeking and waiting when a suddenly happened that shifted the spiritual climate. Let's listen in:

"When the day of Pentecost had come, they were all together in one place. Suddenly a sound like a mighty rushing wind came from heaven, and it filled the whole house where they were sitting. There appeared to them tongues as of fire, being distributed and resting on each of them, and they were all filled with the Holy Spirit and began to speak in other tongues, as the Spirit enabled them to speak" (Acts 2:1-4).

This was the first revival hub—a place of unity where wind and fire suddenly erupted and the people encountered God in a fresh way. They were gloriously filled with the Holy Ghost. Notice the word "suddenly." As Matthew Henry notes in his commentary, this was not a gradual rise of God's Spirit but a sudden fevered pitch of His glory resting upon them. "It came sooner than they expected, and startled even those that were not together waiting, and probably employed in some religious exercises," Henry writes. "It was a sound from heaven, like a thunder-clap."

Doubtless, that religious activity they were engaged in was prayer. As they prayed in unity in their earthly language, the Holy Ghost answered them with tongues like fire that birthed new languages in them—even a heavenly language. They weren't expecting it. They didn't know it was coming. We have an advantage. We have the entire Book of Acts and the Gospels in our hands. We should expect even greater things as we gather in unity and wait on Him in prayer. We should expect spiritual shifts.

In Acts 2, there was a moment in time when the atmosphere changed and a heavenly eruption took place. What was the result? The people shifted as the atmosphere shifted. Fear gave way to bondage-breaking faith. Radical anointing shattered limitations and bondages. In a moment they went from a few disciples tucked away in a quiet room to a revival in the streets bringing in a 3,000-soul harvest. And it wasn't a one-time event. This new and growing revival tribe sustained the shift and saw transforming revival:

"They continued steadfastly in the apostles' teaching and fellowship, in the breaking of bread and in the prayers. Fear came to every soul. And many wonders and signs were done through the apostles. All who believed were together and had all things in common. They sold their property and goods and distributed them to all, according to their need. And continuing daily with one mind in the temple, and breaking bread from house to house, they ate their food with gladness and simplicity of heart, praising God and having favor with all the people. And the Lord added to the church daily those who were being saved" (Acts 2:42-27).

The Holy Spirit is raising up intercessors who are birthing revival hubs that will rise up and shift the spiritual climate in corporate prayer. There's power in corporate unity. There's power in agreement. If one can put 1,000 to flight, two can put 10,000 to flight (see Deuteronomy 32:30). Imagine how many 30 hungry revivalists can put to flight through the power of prayer! Imagine how the spiritual climate could shift if believers gathered in one accord and cooperated with the Holy Spirit!

"Although individuals do have authority, they do not have the level of authority needed to pull down demonic strongholds and territorial spirits over cities and territories," writes Barbara Wentroble in her book Praying With Authority. "A corporate authority is necessary for those tasks. Territorial sprits are fallen angels—principalities, powers, dominions, thrones, authorities and rulers—that exercise influence over cities, regions, even nations. These demonic spirits influence various aspects of culture in much the same way that certain types of soil determine which crops can be grown in particular regions."

PRAISE AND WORSHIP THAT SHIFTS THE ATMOSPHERE

Prayer and worship work hand in hand—and can quickly change the atmosphere in your life. You know this from practical experience. If you are frustrated and upset and you begin to worship God, the atmosphere in your heart changes. You begin to shake off the negative feelings and move in the joy of the Lord. You sense His presence because He inhabits the praises of His people (see Psalm 22:3).

Although we've already discussed prophetic worship in a previous chapter, it's worth exploring praise and worship's ability to set the stage for transforming revival in your region. When David played his harp for Saul, the evil spirit left him (see 1 Samuel 16:23; 1 Samuel 19:9). David shifted the atmosphere with his worship—and so did Paul and Silas after a run in with a Python spirit left them in shackles.

"The crowd rose up together against them. And the magistrates tore the garments off them and gave orders to beat them. After they had laid many stripes on them, they threw them into prison, commanding the jailer to guard them securely. Having received such an order, he threw them into the inner prison and fastened their feet in the stocks. At midnight Paul and Silas were praying and singing hymns to God, and the prisoners were listening to them. Suddenly there was a great earthquake, so that the foundations of the prison were shaken. And immediately all the doors were opened and everyone's shackles were loosened" (Acts 16:22-26).

Talk about shifting the atmosphere! The jailer got saved and so did his entire household. Praise and worship sends confusion into the enemy's camp (see 2 Chronicles 22-23). Aimee Semple McPherson, a Canadian-American evangelist from the 1920s and 1930s—and founder of the Foursquare Church—often conducted faith healing meetings and tens of thousands of people were healed in her meetings. She believed in the power of praise to shift atmospheres. She once wrote:

"The Lord taught me a wonderful lesson some time ago that demonstrated the majesty and power of praise. I was seated on the rostrum in my tent during the evening meeting. Every seat in the big tabernacle was filled, the aisles were packed, and outside the tent hundreds and hundreds stood closely packed together.

"It was one of the first days of the camp meeting, and conviction had not yet taken the place of curiosity. A great many of the onlookers were Roman Catholics, and the balance were unused to any demonstration of the power of God, so the air was filled with unbelief, skepticism, scoffing and ridicule. The people would listen as long as we sang. But as soon as anyone endeavored to speak, the whisperings and the murmurings would begin until another song was started.

"As I stood there on the platform with my eyes closed, I saw the entire tent surrounded by great black demons, with huge, bat-like wings. Each demon seemed to stand about 10 feet tall, and as they stood in a circle, completely surrounding the tent, they were so close together that their wings touched, tip to tip. With my eyes still closed, I began to cry out silently to the Lord, 'Oh, Lord, what shall I do?' He replied, 'Just begin to praise Me. I will do the fighting. You do the praising.' So I began to praise Him.

"Praise the Lord!" The first time I said it I noticed the demons seemed to tremble.

"Praise the Lord!" The second time I shouted it. I am sure my voice was heard above every other sound, and I saw each demon take one step backward, away from the tent.

"Praise the Lord! Praise the Lord! Praise the Lord!" Each time I said, "Praise the Lord," the demons took a step backward until I lost sight of them in the distance.

"Praise the Lord!" The next time I said it I saw in the distance a circular band of angels standing around the tent.

"Praise the Lord! PRAISE THE LORD!" Each time I praised Him they took one step nearer, another step nearer, still another step nearer, till at last they stood at the very border of the tent—such tall, wonderful-looking angels, with their beautiful, white wings spread so wide that the wings of each touched, tip to tip. Father had sent one of His legions of angels to guard the tent.

"Perhaps not another person in the tent saw the vision of this great shining band of angels, yet everyone inside and out must have sensed the presence of the divine, for not only did a great peace steal over my soul, but the whole audience was hushed. When I opened my eyes I could see only the people watching in rapt attention, but when I closed them again I could see the angels just as plainly as I could see the people. Is it any wonder I believe that the power of praise drives back the enemy and brings down the blessing?"

WE'RE RESPONSIBLE FOR THE SPIRITUAL CLIMATE

McPherson demonstrates a valuable lesson. We can influence the spiritual climate. In fact, the spiritual climate in a territory is a direct reflection of the faith and teaching of spiritual pioneers, leaders, and the body of Christ in that region. If an atmosphere is lukewarm it is because that is the standard generations in the territory have set.

Apostolic gifts are sent to pioneer revelation and create a strong, healthy spiritual climate. How we steward the mysteries of God influences our spiritual climates. If the churches in a region only embrace a partial revelation of Jesus—leaving out parts of the gospel—then there will not be a full Kingdom impact. Paul the apostle said, "Let a man so regard us as the ministers of Christ and stewards of the mysteries of God" (1 Corinthians 4:1).

Part of the apostolic call of revival hubs is to steward or manage divine revelation and release that insight to the body in order to establish truth and build faith. The Bible tells us that as a man thinks in his heart, so is he (see Proverbs 23:7). Right living follows right believing. The Word—either through teaching or prophecy—that is declared over a territory has a direct result on the direction of the body of Christ in that territory and the spiritual climate.

We often meet Spirit-filled believers who have chosen to abandon truths they have known and join a ministry that's more comfortable on their flesh. It seems logical that we choose a place where we enjoy fellowshipping. But here's the problem: It matters where we plant our lives and finances matters. The Bible tells us that to whom much is given, much is required (see Luke 12:48). If we partner with ministries that do not promote the full gospel—and establish the truth in a territory when we know the full gospel—then we are intentionally establishing a climate that is not rich with the full flow of God. Believers are responsible for the spiritual climate in their region and they are called to pray, labor, advance and build the Kingdom where they live.

Another problem we have encountered is exhausted pioneers. Men and women who came into a territory proclaiming truth but demonic princes in the region have pounded and wearied them. Too often, this causes worn out pioneers to back off divine truth in order to please people. Pioneers are not sent into the territory to build a fast growing social club but to build a life-giving transformation center. Exhausted pioneers need to get their fire back, shake off the limiting opinions and return to their original vision. Revival hubs provide the reinforcements you need as people of like precious faith fuel one another in God.

Here's the bottom line: The body of Christ is accountable to establish and advance the Kingdom on earth—and that often means shifting spiritual climates. We are privileged God has chosen us to partner with heaven's plans. We pray that God sends people who richly love Jesus and are committed to seeing His dreams fulfilled in the land to regions that need it most—and visits and shakes them with His presence. We're praying for transforming revival—and it begins with shifting spiritual climates. In the next chapter, we'll explore the concept of revival zones.

13

REVIVAL ZONES: TRANSFORMING AND REFORMING CITIES AND REGIONS

Revival for the sake of revival is not enough, nor can nightly revival meetings go on forever without burn out. Revival is unto an awakening that's unto a transformation that's unto a reformation. Not only are the spiritual climates of cities changed, the spheres of society—government, education, media, etc.—are transformed to the glory of God.

We call these revival zones. Revival zones are places of transformational ministry. Let's take a minute to define a "zone" before we forge ahead. Merriam-Webster says a zone is "an area that is different from other areas in a particular way; one of the sections of a city or town that is used for a particular purpose; a region or area set off as distinct from surrounding or adjoining parts."

Wouldn't you like to live, work and worship in an area that's different from the rest of the world, a slice of heaven on earth? Wouldn't you like to see sections of your city or town set apart from God's particular purpose? Wouldn't you like to co-labor with Christ in a region that's distinct to His plans for the next Great Awakening?

Companies of revival-minded believers are arising to dig wells of outpouring in regions. When those wells are dug and the rivers of living water start to flow, the a region is primed not only for revival, but an awakening that spills beyond the four walls of the revival hub and impacts society. Again, transformation is the ultimate goal.

THE MACEDONIAN TRANSFORMATION

You've probably read about the Macedonian cry, sometimes referred to as the Macedonian call, based on Acts 16:9. Would you believe that phrase is actually in Merriam-Webster dictionary? "Macedonian Cry" simply means "an outcry for help." There are regions around the world that are making a Macedonian Cry for revival voices to come into their territories on assignment from God and labor for revival unto awakening unto transformation. Like Paul, these revival voices need to first perceive the call and then obey it. Maybe you are one of them.

Let's look at the encounter in Scripture. When the apostle Paul fell asleep he had no idea he was going to be visited in the night with a prophetic vision to go into Macedonia with the gospel of Christ— he wasn't expecting this Macedonian call. That's often the way it works with revivalists. God calls you to do the unexpected, to go into an unfamiliar territory with a prophetic revelation He's given you to help wake, stir, and bring hope to a city or region.

"During the night a vision appeared to Paul: A man of Macedonia stood and pleaded with him, saying, 'Come over to Macedonia and help us.' After he had seen the vision, immediately we sought to go into Macedonia, concluding that the Lord had called us to preach the gospel to them" (Acts 16:9-11).

The Lord revealed a powerful ministry assignment to Paul. Notice that Paul didn't delay. He immediately obeyed the call and responded to the cry. He was sent to Macedonia to preach the gospel, shift the spiritual climate, win the lost and birth a tremendous transformation. Apostolic ministry brings shift and births transformation in the territory.

Noteworthy is the fact that Paul didn't just go to Macedonia once. He went time and time again—and he sent members of his revival tribe, including Silas, Erastus and Timothy, in and out of Macedonia. If you do a search for Macedonia in Scripture, you'll find it mentioned 25 times. It's clear that some measure of transformation took place on Macedonia because Paul mentions the church there in some of his other epistles.

For example, Paul tells the churches at Thessalonica that they are examples to "all who believe in Macedonia" (see 1 Thessalonians 1:7) and mentions "all the brothers who are in Macedonia" (1 Thessalonians 4:10). Paul also told the church at Corinth that he wanted them to "experience the grace of God bestowed on the churches of Macedonia" (see 2 Corinthians 8:1). Some of the Macedonians also traveled with Paul to other regions (Acts 19:29).

Transformation does happen. George Otis, Jr., president of The Sentinel Group, a Christian research and information agency dedicated to helping the church pray knowledgably for end-time global evangelization and enabling communities to discover the pathway to genuine revival and societal transformation, has studied transformation in over 800 places. He's traveled to six continents in his quest to understand and document true revival—and what we call revival zones.

"Many of these reports stirred my blood—drug cartels being overthrown as Colombian believers gathered in stadiums to pray;

Inuit natives burning fetishes on frozen sea ice as they hear the roaring voice of God; coral reefs springing instantly to life as Fijian villagers rededicated their lives and land to God. These were not the aging stories of revivals long past—they were happening now!" says Otis.

"We think it is society that needs to change," he continues. "But in reality, it is we ourselves—the body of Christ that stand in need of God's touch. For many of us, religious routines have become placeholders for the presence of God. We are doing good things (for God), but not necessarily what He has asked of us. Our love, as the prophet Hosea points out, 'is like the morning mist…that quickly disappears.'

"Transforming revival is not the morning newspaper or a pre-recorded sports event. It is not a product that can be ordered from a catalog, or an experience for which one schedules an appointment. It is not something we can just 'fit in.' If we want to see it, we'll need to cultivate an appetite for it," Otis says. "Satisfaction has been called 'the sleep of prisoners.' At the height of the Hebrides revival, meetings lasted into the wee hours, and crowds often spilled outside the church buildings. On one such occasion, a neighbor lady approached a church elder to complain about the noise. Full of the Holy Spirit, the elder replied: 'Woman, you've slept long enough!'"

CHARACTERISTICS OF REVIVAL ZONES

The church has slept long enough. Revival hubs are laboring in prayer toward transforming revival. Revival hubs cultivate an atmosphere of desperation for God, create a safe place where people can receive a touch from God, encourage believers to love God with all their heart, all the minds, all their soul and all their strength, and stir an appetite for the supernatural, including transforming revival. Revival hubs set free the prisoners of sleep. Revival zones are places of transformational ministry that lead to a transformed people that press into to societal transformation.

Revival zones are home to strong apostolic leadership and apostolic companies that know they have been sent to that particular region with a mandate. They are, effectively, answering a Macedonian Call. People who are laboring to establish a well of revival in a region must identify transformation as the target—not numerical or financial measurements. Often, transformation will be unpopular because it will challenge mindsets and traditions.

Since revelation fuels transformation, preaching and teaching that is full of revelation and heavenly insight fuels revival zones. Plans and purposes for the ministry are birthed in the secret place. Human wisdom does not dominate but heavenly perspective leads. Paul wrote two-thirds of the New Testament by direct revelation from God. The Holy Spirit wants to give us the revelation we need to rebuild the walls in our cities and regions—to build revival zones. David got his blueprints from God, so must revival hub leaders working with the Holy Spirit and revival-minded believers to establish revival zones.

Revival zones are home to revival hubs with strong teaching. Teaching grows and matures a revival zone. Teaching lays solid foundation and releases faith in the hearts of the people. Inspired by the Holy Spirit, Paul admonishes us to "be renewed in the spirit of your mind" (see Ephesians 4:23). Transformation comes in large part by renewing the mind with the Word of God.

RELIGION: AN ENEMY OF REVIVAL

Religion is an enemy of revival. Religion keeps people going through the motions without the life and vitality of the Holy Spirit. Revival zones challenge the religious spirit and loose people to true freedom in Christ. In revival zones, the shackles of lifeless religion are broken. Like revival hubs, revival zones are prayer- and relationship-based. Like revival hubs, revival zones are birthed through prayer and require strong relationships to steward what God is doing in a territory. Unity is vital, because the commanded blessing comes upon spiritual families that are united in love (see Psalm 133:3).

Revival zones embrace the full five-fold ministry and support team ministry with all the gifts active and working together. Revival zones are places of hot pursuit of the Lord—the opposite of comfort zones that maintain the spiritual status quo. Revival zones are continually in motion, flowing the Holy Spirit's instructions and moving with the cloud. Revival zones tap into the power of the media to communicate the gospel and show forth the miraculous works of God. The New Testament is an account of demonstration and transformation. Healing ministries and gospel demonstration are common in revival zones.

Revival zones and works of transformation will require finances. Therefore, there must be teaching on Kingdom wealth and stewardship in revival hubs. There will also be the recognition of a call to entrepreneurship to fund the gospel and do apostolic exploits. A financial mandate and equipping are vital, along with active faith that moves mountains. A revival zone is a place where faith has been taught and activated—and continues to be taught and activated.

Revival zones have a strong prophetic edge. The prophetic anointing is a key element in transforming a territory. Indeed, prophetic gifts are needed to see and sow into the land what the Lord is showing and telling about the land. Prophets and prophetic people sow the Word of the Lord into the land. They declare the promises over the territory. They speak what has been revealed in the secret place. There is great power contained in prophetic proclamation to shift a territory.

The Lord is strategically placing people in territories to bind together and to pray and prophesy over the land. The prophetic has a forerunner heart—running out ahead to release creative words. The realm of prayer lifts us into a place of insight and illumination to see, know and speak. Prophetic prayer that is led by the Holy Spirit and not man's plan is a key weapon in the work of transformation.

This list could go on and on, and at the same time we don't pretend to understand all the nuances of what revival zones will look like as we move forward. But what we do know is this: God is knitting people together for works of transformation in the earth. This will not come without a fight and challenges but Jesus told us that we have authority over the enemy (see Luke 9:1). The greater one is living inside of us and we can walk forward in victory!

Keys to Releasing the Authority of the Lord

Revival zones are often home to more than one revival hub, just like a city is home to more than one church. Revival zones see revival hub leaders working together to establish the full authority and weight of the Kingdom in a territory. As the Kingdom is established, the powers of hell are broken and victory is released. Through prayer, intercession, apostolic building and solid teaching the corporate body of Christ rises to a place of spiritual authority. Here are five keys to releasing the authority of the Lord:

1. Establish the Kingdom: Jesus sent His disciples to preach and release the full weight of the Kingdom. Here are two verses

that demonstrate this reality: "Then He called His twelve disciples together and gave them power and authority over all demons and to cure diseases. And He sent them to preach the kingdom of God and to heal the sick" (Luke 9:1-2) and "Then Jesus came and spoke to them, saying, 'All authority has been given to Me in heaven and on earth. Go therefore and make disciples of all nations, baptizing them in the name of the Father and of the Son and of the Holy Spirit, teaching them to observe all things I have commanded you. And remember, I am with you always, even to the end of the age" (Matthew 28:18-20).

2. Bind the prince over a region: We recognize that principalities, powers and demonic attacks will continue until Satan is cast into the lake of fire but we believe that transforming revival and spiritual warfare can and will push back the darkness. Although people have free wills, we can wrestle the wild beast like Paul (see 2 Corinthians 11:23-29), we can bind and loose (see Matthew 18:18), and we can break demonic influences that work in the sons of disobedience (see Ephesians 2:2) so that people can see the light of the gospel.

3. Govern in prayer: There is a realm of prayer that releases the government of God and binds the powers of hell. True government in the world takes place in prayer. Jesus said, "I will give you the keys of the kingdom of heaven, and whatever you bind on earth shall be bound in heaven, and whatever you loose on earth shall be loosed in heaven" (Matthew 16:17-21). Jesus also taught us to pray, "Your kingdom come; Your will be done on earth, as it is in heaven" (Matthew 6:10). We govern in prayer by praying to God what He tells us to

pray.

4. Release the King Of Glory: Worship builds His throne. God inhabits the praises of His people (see Psalm 22:3). Psalm 24:7-8 declares, "Lift up your heads, O you gates; and be lifted up, you everlasting doors, that the King of glory may enter. Who is this King of glory? The Lord strong and mighty, the Lord mighty in battle." The sounds of revival and awakening are key in revival zones. The hungry cry out.

5. Renew the corporate mind with teaching, tearing down strongholds and break man-made, legalistic traditions: Again, the ministry of teaching is critical! Establishing proper belief systems fuels revival and a release of the power of God. James Chapter 3 speaks of the need to tame the tongue and receive the wisdom that is from above.

If the Lord has given you a vision for a region, hold on! Keep birthing it in the secret place. Hold that vision near to your heart and allow the wind of God to breath upon it. Let's press, pray, build and advance! In the next chapter, we'll draw lessons from Nehemiah's exploit to rebuild the walls.

14

A NEHEMIAH COMPANY OF REVIVAL HUB BUILDERS ON THE WALL

The Lord is raising up a Nehemiah Company in this hour—a people who will build revival hubs according to His pattern and release His plan for awakening in the nations. Just like David got the building plans for the temple from God—and passed it on to his son Solomon—the Holy Spirit is giving revival-minded leaders building plans for revival hubs that can host His glory (see 1 Chronicles 28).

We've said this before—but it bears repeating—there is no cookie cutter approach to revival hubs. Although there are principles that we've laid out throughout this book, there are many different expressions, or flavors, of revival hubs. The expression depends in large part on two factors: the territory in which you are building and the gift mix of the leadership.

For example, some revival hubs are worship-centric while others are warfare-centric. Some revival hubs may carry a governmental mantle while others carry a healing mantle. Some revival hubs are intercession-focused while others are heavier on teaching. All revival hubs will emphasize worship, intercession, teaching and the supernatural, then, but depending on what the region needs and the giftings of the leader, the expression may have a dominant flow. This is part of the pattern God has given the leader for building.

The expression is up to God, and so is the grace to build. As a Nehemiah company, we must rely on the power of God to build. Indeed, the word of the Lord to Zerubbabel applies to anyone building a revival hub—or anything else—in the Kingdom of God: "Not by might nor by power, but by My Spirit, says the Lord of Hosts" (Zechariah 4:6).

THE BURDEN TO BUILD

Before you can assemble a Nehemiah company, you must receive the burden of the Lord to build. We discussed this calling in a previous chapter but it bears repeating here. Building a revival hub is not for the faint of heart. It's likely that you will not get any cooperation—and, in fact, may be persecuted—by the church establishment. If you are not burdened by the condition of the church—if you are not burdened the enemy's plans to ruin America—don't build a revival hub. Nehemiah started with a burden. We read about it in Nehemiah 1:1-10:

"In the month Kislev, in the twentieth year, while I was in Susa the palace, Hanani, one of my relatives, and some men of Judah arrived. So I asked them concerning the returning Jews who had been in captivity, and concerning Jerusalem. They said to me, 'The remnant that returned from captivity is there in the province enduring great affliction and reproach. Also, the wall of Jerusalem remains broken down, and its gates have been burned with fire.' When I heard these words, I sat down and wept and mourned for days. Then I fasted, and prayed before the God of heaven, and said:

"I beseech You, O Lord God of heaven, the great and awesome God, who keeps covenant and mercy for those who love Him and keep His commandments. Let Your ear now be attentive, and Your eyes open, that You may hear the prayer of Your servant, which I now pray before You, day and night, for the children of Israel Your servants, and confess the sins of the children of Israel, which we have sinned against You. Both my father's house and I have sinned. We have acted very corruptly against You and have not obeyed the commandments, nor the statutes, nor the judgments, which You commanded Your servant Moses.

"Please remember the word that You commanded Your servant Moses, saying, 'If you behave unfaithfully, then I will scatter you among the nations, but if you return to Me and keep My commandments and do them, though your outcasts are under the farthest part of the heavens, I will gather them from there and bring them back to the place where I have chosen to establish My name.'

"Now these are Your servants and Your people, whom You have redeemed by Your great power and by Your strong hand. O Lord, I implore You, let Your ear be attentive to the prayer of Your servant, and to the prayer of Your servants who delight to revere Your name. And let Your servant prosper this day, and grant him mercy in the sight of this man."

BUILDING WITH FAVOR

If you have a burden to build, the favor of the Lord will be upon you to execute the vision. But you also need favor with people. As Solomon put it, you need, "favor and good understanding in the sight of God and man" (Proverbs 3:4). As you're making intercession over the burden to build and pressing into get the blueprint from God, also pray for favor. Nehemiah had great favor, and you will need the same. Psalm 5:12 offers this promise you can pray: "For You, Lord, will bless the righteous; You surround him with favor like a shield."

Nehemiah, the king's cupbearer, clearly had supernatural favor with the king. As the story goes, he king saw that Nehemiah looked troubled and asked him what was wrong. He told the king that the city, the place of his father's tombs, was laying in waste and its gates were destroyed by fire (see Nehemiah 2:3). The king asked him what he could do to help. Nehemiah "immediately" prayed to God and then asked the king for help. We read the encounter in Nehemiah 2:4-8:

"If this pleases the king and if this might be good for your servant who is before you, then would you send me to Judah, to the city of my fathers' tombs so that I may rebuild it?" The king, with the queen sitting beside him, said to me, 'How long would your journey be? And when will you return?' Because it pleased the king to send me, I established a timetable for him.

"I further said to the king, 'If this pleases the king, may letters be given to me for the governors of the province Beyond the River so that they would allow me to pass through until I come to Judah, as well as a letter to Asaph the keeper of the king's forest, that he may give me timber to make beams for the gates of the temple mount, for the city wall, and for the house into which I will enter.' The king granted me these things, because the good hand of my God was upon me."

If God has called you to build a revival hub—whether you are the leader or part of the company—press into the favor of God with your city, with churches, with people who have resources to help the cause and everybody else. Let Psalm 90:17 be your prayer: "Let the beauty of the Lord our God be upon us, and establish the work of our hands among us; yes, establish the work of our hands."

GUARD THE VISION

If God is calling you to build a revival hub, it's best not to rush out and begin sharing the vision with anyone and everyone. Many people will not understand this new paradigm and may try to talk you out of it before you ever get started. On the other hand, you aren't called to do this alone—but you don't need hundreds of people to launch, either. Jesus turned the world upside down with 12 disciples.

Share your vision only with those who are closely aligned with you and pray together about moving forward. At the beginning, there were only a few men with Nehemiah, but little is much when God is in it. Micro is the new mega when God is on your side. Special forces are arising focused on big assignments with a chosen few that will eventually lead a great army into awakening. Look at Nehemiah's strategy in Nehemiah 2:11-18:

"When I arrived in Jerusalem, I was there three days. Then I arose in the night, I and a few men who were with me; I told no one what my God had put in my heart to do for Jerusalem. There was no animal with me, except the one on which I rode.

"So I went out by night by the Valley Gate toward the Dragon's Well and then to the Dung Gate, because I was inspecting the broken-down walls of Jerusalem and its burned gates. Next I passed by the Fountain Gate and then to the King's Pool, but there was no place for my mount to pass. By going up along the riverbed at night, I inspected the wall. Then I turned back so that I could enter by the Valley Gate, and then came back again. 16 The officials did not know where I went or what I did, since I had not yet told it to the Jews, the priests, the nobles, the officials, or to any of the others who would do the work.

"Finally, I said to them, 'You see the distress that we are in, how Jerusalem is devastated and its gates are burned with fire. Come, and let us rebuild the wall of Jerusalem so that we will no more be a reproach.' Then I told them that the hand of my God had been good to me and also about the king's words that he had spoken to me. And they said, 'Let us rise up and build!' So they strengthened their hands for the good work."

Nehemiah gave the charge. We must hear the Lord's charge in this hour. Jesus said, "He who has ears to hear, let him hear" (Matthew 11:15). The Lord is raising up a prophetic partnership with the apostolic to see, know, rise and build with favor.

Don't Let Sanballat Stop You!

When God called me (Jennifer) to build our revival hub, I knew it would come with opposition. I'll admit, I never thought it would play out with literal Sanballats. But that's just what has happened—and often these Sanballats come in sheep's clothing.

Sanballat is an enemy of revival and brings strong opposition to what God wants to build. Sanballat is a critical persecutor who brings false accusations against the work and the people putting their hand to the plow. And Sanballat will rally others to the opposition against you, like Tobiahs and Geshems, just like he did to Nehemiah.

The spirit of Sanballat's goal is to discourage you—to get you to quit what God has called you to do. This spirit's overarching mission is to thwart God's work. It's a judgmental, mocking, insidious spirit that, again, sometimes comes in sheep's clothing. Someone flowing in this spirit may even offer to come alongside and help you, but its intentions are to tear down—not build up—the figurative wall God is calling you to build.

Since I opened the doors to Awakening House of Prayer, I've encountered a trio of "Sanballats." All three initially presented as sold out, on fire intercessors with a passion to build the house of prayer. But, soon enough, all three manifested their true intentions: to distract the builders from God's work. These deceived Sanballats may not even realize they are on an assignment from the evil one.

The first Sanballat came in with a commitment to pray five days a week. That lasted about a month before the truth manifested. When impure motives came to the light leadership called him out. That's when the Sanballat spirit took its mask off and began persecuting, bringing false accusations, and calling down God's judgment. He tried to rally others to his side but God frustrated his purposes and he faded out as quickly as appeared on the scene.

The second Sanballat came in with the line "You need me! You can't do this without me!" She was actually faithful to pray and even help with administrative work in the beginning. But soon enough she began criticizing the model and the leadership. The false accusations were much more subtle, laced with feigned sincerity, but they were accusations nonetheless. This Sanballat left for another prayer ministry she felt could bring her more recognition.

The third Sanballat was almost identical. She came in with a commitment to pray five days a week. She never did fulfill that commitment. It was a lot of talk and inconsistent action, along with a critical, presumptuous spirit. When corrected, the false accusations came flowing in against leadership. When those accusations went unanswered, this spirit influenced her to "declare war" and demand a position in the house of prayer.

DEALING WITH THE SANBALLAT SPIRIT

Maybe you recognize this Sanballat spirit flowing in your midst. Any time you set out to build something for God, you will find enemy opposition. So how do you handle the spirit of Sanballat? Do what Nehemiah did.

When Sanballat, Tobiah and Geshem heard about Nehemiah's plans to rebuild the Jerusalem wall, they were at first grieved. When they saw Nehemiah was executing his vision, they laughed him to scorn, despised the builders and accused them of rebelling against the king (see Neh. 2:19).

Nehemiah's answer: "Then answered I them and said to them, 'The God of heaven, He will enable us to prosper. Therefore we His servants will arise and build, but you will have no portion, or right, or memorial in Jerusalem" (Neh. 2:20). Don't shrink back from confronting this spirit with the truth of God's Word. If you are confident in what God has called you to do, stand and build despite the scorners, despisers and accusers. And don't give them the right to build alongside you—or to speak into the work.

When Sanballat heard that Nehemiah and his crew were making progress on the wall, he was furious, indignant and began mocking the Jews. Sanballat and his clan began speaking against the work. Nehemiah 4:1-3 shows the attack:

"When Sanballat heard that we were rebuilding the wall, he became angry and was greatly irritated, and he mocked the Jews. He spoke before his relatives and the army of Samaria and said, 'What are these feeble Jews doing? Are they fortifying themselves? Will they make sacrifices? Can they complete this in a day? Can they revive the burned-up stones out of the rubbish heaps?' Now Tobiah the Ammonite was beside him, and he said, 'Even what they are rebuilding, if even a fox climbed it, that would break down their stone wall.'"

Sanballat didn't stop with the word curses. No, he also conspired to attack the work. Nehemiah 4:6-8 reveals:

"So we rebuilt the wall until all of it was solidified up to half its height. The people had a passion for the work. When Sanballat, Tobiah, the Arabians, the Ammonites, and the Ashdodites heard how the restoration of Jerusalem's walls was progressing and how the breaches had begun to be sealed, it made them extremely furious. So they all conspired together to fight against Jerusalem in order to cause it chaos."

Even after the wall was rebuilt, Sanballat didn't give up. His demonic clan still sought to bring harm. Nehemiah 6:1-3 tells us:

"When Sanballat, Tobiah, Geshem the Arabian, and the rest of our enemies heard that I had rebuilt the wall and that there was not a gap in it (though at that time I had not erected the doors on the gates), Sanballat and Geshem sent to me, saying, 'Come, that we might meet together in one of the villages in the plain of Ono.' But they planned to do evil to me. So I sent messengers to them, saying, 'I am doing a great work, so I am not able to come down. Why should the work cease while I leave it and come down to you?'"

Sanballat's nonsense did not distract Nehemiah. He stayed focused on erecting the gates. As a matter of fact, he didn't even go deal with his detractors face to face. Stubborn Sanballat continued demanding a meeting with Nehemiah. The Bible says he sent the same message to Nehemiah four times and four times Nehemiah offered the same response. Sanballat then started making false accusations against Nehemiah and his motives and appointed prophets to spread lies about him (Neh. 6:6-7) in attempts to scare him away from the work. Sanballat was trying to force him out of own ministry!

Nehemiah's response: He ignored the threats and put it in God's hands: "Remember, O my God, concerning Tobiah and Sanballat these deeds of theirs, as well as the prophetess Noadiah and the rest of the prophets who were trying to frighten me" (Neh. 6:14).

DON'T STOP GOD'S WORK!

Finally, the wall was built. But it could have turned out another way if Nehemiah wasn't resolute in his mission. Again, any time you set out to build something for God, you will find enemy opposition.

Of course, it won't always be Sanballat, although this spirit is one that takes aim at builders of the wall and repairers of the breach. Many times it's religious spirits or Jezebel spirits that try to infiltrate the work God has called you to do. In my Sanballat experiences, Jezebel and religion also joined in the assault.

Ultimately, the response is similar: Be led by the Holy Spirit as to when to confront and when to disregard the enemy's accusations. Be led by the Holy Spirit as to when to meet with your persecutors and when to send messengers to deal with them. But whatever you do, don't stop God's work! Amen. In our final chapter, we'll dive into the concept of laying the foundation for generational revival.

15

Laying the Foundation for Generational Revival

Revival hubs do not operate with a one-man-only paradigm, nor do they die out when the leadership goes on to glory. Revival hub leadership prepares a people for generational revival—a revival culture or awakening that lasts beyond a generation. Think about it for a minute. The First Great Awakening broke the church out of established church doctrine boxes by emphasizing individual faith and salvation. New denominations were birthed out of the First Great Awakening, which lasted over 20 years. That's not quite a generation but consider that the Second Great Awakening lasted 50 years and you start to get a glimpse of generational revival.

The Second Great Awakening turned outward and focused on evangelism. Up until this time, Congregationalists and Anglicans were the largest presence in America, but the Second Great Awakening saw the rise of the Methodists and Baptists. Camp meetings with thousands, including a revival at the Cane Ridge meeting house in Paris, Kentucky in 1802 that saw 20,000 people, took place around the nation.

Because it lasted over a generation, the Second Great Awakening shifted America's religious landscape like nothing else up until that point. It was an evangelical movement that shunned Calvinistic tradition and emphasized that people could exercise their free will and believe in the Son of God unto salvation. The Second Great Awakening also opened the door to more women and African-Americans.

Instead of generational curses, what if we could see generational revivals? We know it's possible because God has done it before—but it's rare. Generational revival depends, at least in some measure, on the generations connecting. In a generational revival, we may express a move of God in different ways but we are joined together, honoring one another, to press into the same move. We a generational transfer of spiritual wealth, so to speak.

In his book Jesus Culture: Living a Life that Transforms the World, Banning Liebscher, co-director of Jesus Culture, shares a revelation that we should all grasp:

"I must take what I received for free—paid for by another man— and steward it in such a way that it increases and more revelation is added. I must fight my own battles, not only to keep the revelation I was given, but to steward it in such a way that it increases in my care. The spirit of independence has deceived us into thinking we need to strive on our own and learn things by ourselves, so we end up only reaching as far as those before us. Rather than working from the same floor in the building of revival that my fathers and mothers have built, I want to take what they've received and propel it to the next level. And that is what they want for me."

RESISTING THE EMERGING MOVE OF GOD

Younger believers need to honor the generals of the faith that went before them, but mature Christians also need to recognize, encourage and equip the gifts of believers coming after them. It's more than the proverbial passing of the baton. Spiritual fathers and sons—spiritual mothers and daughters—need to run together before the baton is handed over. This is especially true in the context of generational revival.

Unfortunately, the greatest opponents to an emerging move of God are often those who pioneered the last move of God. That is usually because the Spirit of God doesn't move the same way He did last time around. Many people who embraced even the most unusual moves of the Spirit—and who stood in the face of persecution for their radical faith—resist or reject an emerging move.

King Saul is one example in Scripture that shows the extremes of this mindset. Saul not only fought against David—he wanted to kill him. Saul did everything in his power to hinder the emergence of a fresh prophetic leader that was anointed to take the baton. Saul had a religious spirit, which is an enemy of revival. Saul also tapped into a spirit of fear. This combination motivated him to attack David.

"It came to pass the following day, that an evil spirit from God came upon Saul, so that he raved in the midst of the house. And David was playing the lyre, as at other times. Now there was a spear in Saul's hand. And Saul threw the spear. For he said, 'I will pin David to the wall.' But David avoided him two times. Saul was afraid of David because the Lord was with him but had departed from Saul. Therefore Saul removed him from his presence and placed him as his captain over a thousand. And he went out and came in before the people. David was successful in all his ways and the Lord was with him. When Saul saw that he was very successful, he was afraid of him. Now all Israel and Judah loved David, because he went out and came in before them" (1 Samuel 18:10-16).

Saul positioned himself like a wall to hold back the next move of God instead of a gateway to release the move with his blessing. The Bible says Saul was actually afraid of David and demoted him when God was trying to raise him up. Saul and David should have been working together, but Saul would not have it. Later in Scripture we see that Saul tried to kill David, but David continued to honor God's anointed. Our prayer is that the leaders of the last great move of God would enter into the next great move of God instead so the generations can run together.

Leaders over ministries and churches should be the catalyst for revival—not the opponents of it. Leaders of true revival hubs—not revival hubs in name only—have a heart for the next great move of God and seek to impart, empower, equip, activate and release everyone in the hub to do what God has called them to do (even if it means leaving to start another revival hub). There is no competition in the revival hub setting, but rather cooperation, teamwork and partnerships. Revival hubs are atmospheres where iron sharpens iron (see Proverbs 27:17). Personal victories and advances are celebrated because when one member of the body wins, we all win.

IDENTIFYING THE NEXT GENERATION OF REVIVALISTS

God gave Elijah the prophetic assignment of identifying the next great prophet. The Lord said to him, "Go, return on the road through the Wilderness of Damascus, and when you arrive, anoint Hazael to be king over Aram. And you shall anoint Jehu, the son of Nimshi, to be king over Israel, and you shall anoint Elisha, the son of Shaphat of

Abel Meholah, to be prophet in your place" (1 Kings 19:15-16).

Can you imagine? For some leaders, that would be a hard pill to swallow. This prophetic directive came just after Elijah had killed the 850 false prophets; right after Jezebel sent a messenger of fear that caused him to take off running into the wilderness; right after God corrected him for his self-righteous attitude that he was the only prophet of the Lord in the land. Elijah could have sulked about it this transition of power. But rather than being fearful and intimidated—or disobeying God's command—Elijah embraced the assignment and fathered his successor. This is the model of the emerging move—ministry gifts pouring into those who will arise and lead the next move.

"Still, I have preserved seven thousand men in Israel for Myself, all of whose knees have not bowed to Baal and whose mouths have not kissed him. So he departed from there and found Elisha the son of Shaphat, who was plowing with twelve yoke of oxen before him and he with the twelfth, and Elijah passed by him and threw his cloak on him" (1 Kings 19:18-19).

The release of true prophetic ministry opens the eyes of believers to find their assigned place. Paul prayed as an apostolic father that the eyes of the church be opened so that we could know the place, position that God has called us to:

"Therefore I also, after hearing of your faith in the Lord Jesus and your love toward all the saints, do not cease giving thanks for you, mentioning you in my prayers, so that the God of our Lord Jesus Christ, the Father of glory, may give you the Spirit of wisdom and revelation in the knowledge of Him, that the eyes of your understanding may be enlightened, that you may know what is the hope of His calling and what are the riches of the glory of His inheritance among the saints, and what is the surpassing greatness of His power toward us who believe, according to the working of His mighty power, which He performed in Christ when He raised Him from the dead and seated Him at His own right hand in the heavenly places, far above all principalities, and power, and might, and dominion, and every name that is named, not only in this age but also in that which is to come. And He put all things in subjection under His feet and made Him the head over all things for the church, which is His body, the fullness of Him who fills all things in all ways" (Ephesians 1: 15:23).

Revival hubs are a safe place for all generations. Revival hubs embrace the spiritual fathers and mothers and the spiritual sons and daughters. As we explained in the chapter on revival tribes, revival hubs are home to a spiritual family. This spiritual family celebrates together, grieves together, wars together, and wants to see the next generation move to deeper and higher levels in God to usher in a fresh outpouring that continues to transform a region with God's glory.

ELISHA'S BOLD GENERATIONAL REQUEST

When the time came for Elijah to go on to glory, he wanted to make sure his spiritual son had everything he needed to succeed in carrying his calling. He may not have expected Elisha to be so bold, but notice in these verses how he did not squash the young man's enthusiasm. Notice how Elijah nurtured the passion and told him what was possible instead of what was impossible.

"And as they were crossing, Elijah said to Elisha, 'Ask for something, and I will do it for you before I am taken away from you.' And Elisha said, 'Let a double portion of your spirit be upon me.' He said, 'You have asked for a difficult thing, but if you see me when I am taken from you, it will happen to you. If not, it will not.'" (2 Kings 2:9-10).

Elijah encouraged the hunger in Elisha—and even stirred it up, challenging his faith to continue pursuing until the end. Paul did something similar with his spiritual son Timothy. He told him, "Therefore I remind you to stir up the gift of God, which is in you by the laying on of my hands. For God has not given us the spirit of fear, but of power, and love, and self-control" (2 Timothy 1:6-7).

Unlike Saul, Elijah and Paul were not scared of the next generation but wanted to see them lead a new move of God. As a faithful son, Elisha pressed into his inheritance blessing so he could complete the course and finish his spiritual assignment.

"As they continued walking and talking, a chariot of fire and horses of fire separated the two of them, and Elijah went up by a whirlwind into heaven. Elisha was watching and crying, 'My father, my father, the chariot of Israel and its horsemen!' And he did not see him again. Then he grabbed his own clothes and tore them in two pieces. He picked up the robe of Elijah that fell from him, and he returned and stood on the bank of the Jordan. And he took the robe of Elijah that fell from him, and struck the water, and said, 'Where is the Lord, God of Elijah?' When he had struck the water, it parted from one side to the other, and Elisha crossed over" (2 Kings 2:11-14).

The deepest impartation—the double portion—is reserved for spiritual sons and daughters. Paul longed to see his spiritual children so that he could impart some spiritual gift that would strengthen them (see Romans 1:11). Paul imparted much, and it's most obvious in the life of Timothy. Paul said of him, "Therefore I have sent Timothy to you. He is my beloved son and is faithful in the Lord. He will remind you of my ways which are in Christ, as I teach everywhere in every church" (1 Corinthians 4:17).

Like Elisha, sons and daughters must pursue fathers and mothers—and sow honor. Spiritual sons should respect and honor their spiritual fathers, according to Peter Sumrall, the son of Dr. Lester Sumrall. That means serving the father's vision and taking his advice concerning your own. "My dad used to laugh because some guys would say 'You are my spiritual father,' but they were too busy to pick him up at the airport," Sumrall recalls. "They didn't understand the meaning of serving, or of receiving the spiritual insight and authority a father has to offer."

By the same token, ministers must value the mantle of fathering and mothering. This is a true paradigm shift in the body of Christ. The Baby Boomer generation didn't have many fathers and so many did not know how to father Generation X. Nevertheless, Generation X must rise up and answer the call to father the Millennnials. Revival hubs foster a culture that values spiritual relationships. Revival hubs are fathering houses filled with sons and daughters who value relationship above opportunity and understand that every spiritual relationship and assignment carries a reward.

Revival hubs are stewarding a multi-generational movement. The establishment of the Kingdom demands spiritual fathers who are willing to propel their spiritual sons to greater heights. Dough Stringer, founder of Somebody Cares America, puts it this way: "We will either be like Elizabeth rejoicing over the birthing of a forerunner generation or we will be like Rachael weeping over the loss of a whole generation. It is up to us as the church to carry the expression of Christ and to really represent the Father to a generation that has been deemed fatherless."

ABOUT THE AUTHORS

Jennifer LeClaire is senior editor of Charisma. She is also director of Awakening House of Prayer, Awakening Healing Rooms and Bound4LIFE in Fort Lauderdale, Florida, co-founder of AwakeningTV.com, a digital based media production to host revival inspired services, ministers and messages both past and current. She also serves on the leadership team of the New Breed Revival Network. She is ordained by Network Ekklessia International, an apostolic network founded by Dutch Sheets. She is the author of dozens of books, including *The Next Great Move of God: An Appeal to Heaven for Spiritual Awakening; Mornings With the Holy Spirit, Listening Daily to the Still, Small Voice of God; The Making of a Prophet and Satan's Deadly Trio: Defeating the Deceptions of Jezebel, Religion and Witchcraft.* Some of her materials have been translated into Spanish, Portuguese and Korean.

Visit her online at jenniferleclaire.org.

Ryan LeStrange began in ministry after training under his spiritual father, Dr. Norvel Hayes. The apostolic call on his life led him to build multiple ministries in various geographical locations, the foremost being Ryan LeStrange Ministries. Ryan, a modern-day Revivalist, moves strongly in the power of God, traveling the globe to ignite Revival Fires. His crusades and services are alive with Prophetic declaration, miracles and healings, and powerful preaching.

Ryan is one of the senior leaders of New Breed Revival Network, a network of ministers committed to see Revival birthed in America and the nations. He is co-founder of AwakeningTV.com, a media channel created to host revival inspired services, featuring ministers and messages both past and present. Ryan has authored several books and is presently working on several more. *The Fire of Revival* and *Releasing the Prophetic* have inspired believers to press for more of God. He is the founder and Apostle of Impact International Apostolic Fellowship, an organization created to father and network ministers around the world.

Ryan and his wife Joy currently reside in Abingdon, Virginia.